Ethyle

The Rise and Fall of the 139th Street NFL Crew

Lou Black

Respect the Pen LLC

Ethylene: The Rise and Fall of the 139th Street NFL Crew is a work of nonfiction. Some names and identifying details have been changed.

1

Dedication

If someone you love ever picked up a drug to sell or a gun to shoot, this book is dedicated to you. Losing them to the prison system or worse, the grave, is a burden left for you to carry for eternity. May you somehow find the necessary solace when it becomes too much to bear. And may God bless you all.

Table of Contents

We've all heard the saying "one bad apple spoils the whole bunch," and have probably seen instances where it does apply to people, but does it actually happen to fruit? Yes. As they ripen, some fruits, like apples and pears, produce a gaseous hormone called ethylene, which is among other things, a ripening agent."

eth•yl•ene
eTHəlēn
noun: **ethylene**

> a flammable hydrocarbon gas of the alkene series, occurring in natural gas, coal gas, and crude oil and given off by ripening fruit. It is used in chemical synthesis.

Destiny is a matter of choice, not chance.

-Charlamagne Thagod

Prologue

First and foremost, I would like to say R.I.P. to the four fallen characters in these writings. I would also like to extend my deepest heartfelt condolences to their families. The purpose of these writings is by no means intended to offend, insult, discredit, or defame anyone. My motives are pure with no malice directed toward anyone.

Having said that, remember that I'm human and I make mistakes. If I cause anyone to feel slighted, I apologize in advance. I'm offering my unbiased version of the truth as I know it. While I express my opinion, I welcome you, the reader, the option of formulating your own opinion at the end. I also ask that I be excused for any inaccuracies or omissions that may be found in these writings.

I wasn't always afforded access to certain information because of where I sit in this narrative. Not everyone will agree with the contents of this book and that is perfectly acceptable. The words you are about to read are not based on my opinion of actual events, they are factual. Some names have been modified or omitted to protect identities and maintain privacy.

While I attempted to tell this story as accurately possible, some may feel offended, so I was compelled to offer this disclaimer. Those who know the story will know who's who. Others will have to decipher it on their own.

I had to make the difficult choice to provide the reader with a diluted version to avoid facing libel suits. For the reader who wanted it in its purest form, I offer my sincere apologies. Some may ask how I can be unbiased when I'm closely related to one of the deceased. While one of the deceased is a relative and his death caused me a great deal of pain, the demise of the other three hurt just as much. There was a time when I loved them all equally. That love was based on brotherhood and loyalty. It was a loyalty that demanded that I put my gun in my hand and ride for any and all members of my crew, whether a blood relative or not.

If I took a bullet for my family, would I bleed differently had it been for another NFL member? If I fired my gun and went to prison for my family, would the years behind bars feel any different than if it were for someone else from the block? I don't have to answer these questions for you. Any real mf knows the answers. Of course I had a special love for my cousin, while loving my NFL family too. That's just who I am. I know I speak for myself and others when I say I would've risked my freedom and even my very own life for anyone in my crew. I put that on the souls of my grandchildren and no one can dispute that!

That's how we rolled back then. Unity was our biggest strength and we lived by it. Some may ask, "Who do you think you are, writing this story?" Who am I? I am an original NFL member, not an affiliate or associate. My involvement wasn't by chance. It was hands-on, in the battlefield and in the trenches if needed. That gives me the right to speak my piece. Their story is my story. Their highs were my highs; their lows, my lows. I can speak it because I lived, breathed, and felt it along with them. I still do.

I have to admit, I started writing as a form of therapy. I shed many tears, and expressing myself through the written word has proved to be an effective coping mechanism. It was, and still is, very difficult for me. My mother asked why I decided to write this book. She expressed concern because some people may or not like what I have to say. My response: "Those people should be glad I'm writing a book instead of handling it in the street."

If this were twenty-five years ago I would probably be in jail by now, by reacting without thinking. Now left to wrestle with thoughts of revenge every day, I asked my mother to pray for me and ask God to remove the hatred from my heart because grief was going to force me to do something crazy. Notice I said crazy, not regretful. I attribute my decision of not wilding out to age and wisdom.

Over the years, maturity has shown me I have way too much to live for. More importantly, I'd like to do my part to break the cycle of the senseless killing of black men. The system doesn't need our help. It's taken everything in me to swallow this last loss but I feel I have to be the bigger man.

Therefore, I write.

So come with me. Follow along and be prepared as I take you on the journey of these four individuals who considered themselves brothers, and the story of how they succumbed to the pitfalls street life had to offer.

This is the tale of the 139th St. NFL Crew and their rise and inevitable fall on the streets of Harlem.

Introduction

1967-1997

1969-2002

1970-2016

1974-1999

Never in a million years did I think these dates would become as significant as they did, involving four people I knew and loved my whole life. Their deaths would change the dynamic of an entire crew, including their families, forever.

This is the story of a group of kids who grew into men, together living on one block, navigating the ins and outs of drugs and murder on the streets of Harlem. One street in particular is where jealousy, envy, and revenge all collided and brought a crew to its knees. It divided the block and turned what had once been peaceful families into enemies forever.

This is the street where I'm from.

This is the street where we were born and raised, and those that had been my friends and family ultimately met their violent demise.

The street I will always love but now simultaneously hate.

This is 139th and Lenox.

This is The Danger Zone.

Matthew "Reggie" White

1967-1997

Some may know how the story ended, but most don't know the way it began. The beginning was a simpler time where love, loyalty, and happiness was the order of the day. Growing up in the seventies and eighties in Harlem was rough at times but we managed to make it through. Well, most of us.

While a lot of our homes were governed by single mothers raising multiple children, Reg (short for Reggie) was one of the fortunate ones. He had both parents at home, along with three sisters. As idyllic as this sounds, I'm pretty sure they had their share of hardship. Thomas "TC" Riley and Gerard "Gee Love" Woodley lived with their mom in the same house where she grew up in as a child herself. Their mom is my mother's younger sister and she did the best she could to make ends meet as any responsible parent would.

Leroy "Lee" Phinazee, on the other hand, had it a little different; his mom, although a single parent as well, went the extra mile to provide for her three boys. Lee was the middle child, Donald "Don" Phinazee, the oldest, and Lamont Coleman, the youngest, who the world would come to know as "Big L." While technically Lamont was the boys' cousin, their mom took him in and raised him as her own.

She was a hustler who did what she had to in order to provide the life she saw fit for her three young princes. I won't get into specifics but she didn't sell drugs or disrespect her body as some may have done. She did very well by her boys and not only just for them. She loved all the kids on the block. Not only did she do things like hold a seat on the block association and organize block parties, but she took

10

things a step further and did things like sponsor trips to amusement parks for us all. We loved it and we all loved *her*. She was the type of person who was good to everyone she encountered on 139th Street.

I wish I could truly convey how it was growing up on our block. There was an abundance of love and unity. While I don't doubt other blocks around Harlem may have been similar, I can only speak about what I know.

Lee and his brothers always had just a little more than most kids on the block. They stayed fresh with the latest fashions and whatever was hot at the time was what they had. British Walkers, Bally's, AJ's, Overlaps, Pro Keds, you name it, they had it. They were the first family on the block to have a Betamax machine and when VHS technology came out they were the first to upgrade. They had so many VHS tapes, they could've opened a Blockbuster Video (you get the idea).

With all the things Lee possessed, he still found reason to display an air of antagonism. If someone had a new pair of sneakers, he would step on them to purposely try and mess them up. If you had a new jacket, Lee would grab it and wrinkle it. For the life of me, I couldn't figure out why, but that's what he did.

Most of us weren't bothered by his ways; there was no time for jealousy and pettiness back then. We all played, laughed, and snapped on each other like all kids did. Of course, there were arguments and an occasional fight; I mean, we didn't live on Sesame Street. Any disagreements were all but forgotten and back to normal in a day or two; that's just the way it was. The way it was supposed to be.

Teenage years were soon upon us. Most people from the block attended Julia Richman High School but there were a few exceptions. Reg went to Louis D. Brandeis, while TC and Gee went to A. Philip

Randolph Campus High School and Lamont attended Park West High School. I personally went to Thomas A. Edison High School in Queens. My early years were spent growing up in the East New York section of Brooklyn. Although I was born on 139th Street, my mother moved to Brooklyn when I was four years old, but I never really identified with the BK (Brooklyn) way of life. I was Harlem all the way and broke my neck to get my ass uptown every chance I got. There was something about Harlem that called to me. I just had to be there. When I turned 18, I moved back to my aunt's house on 139th Street, leaving Brooklyn in the dust.

Things start to change in all teens as their bodies and minds transition to young adulthood. You see things differently. You feel differently about life. One tries to see where they fit in and how to find their place in the world. What path will you take on the journey into manhood? Do you finish high school and get a job? (Hopefully one that pays the bills) Or, will you take the so called 'easy route?' It's said that choosing street life is 'the easy way,' but I tend to disagree. The money may be faster and more plentiful in the street but by no means is it easier. There's so much more at stake when you indulge in street activity. You have to watch for the police first and foremost. Second, is the stickup man. Then, in some cases, your own family and friends might be envious of you. That has to be a terrible feeling, to be betrayed by someone close. Sad to say, it happens, as you shall soon see.

Needless to say, most of us didn't take the legal route.1986 was the year most of us dove headfirst into the crack game, everyone except Rich Dice.(We call each other, "Twin" because people say we resemble one another so much) He was the first one in our age group from 139thStreet to ever sell drugs. And he didn't even sell it. Twin started as a lookout for a crew out of 140th Street between 7th and 8th Avenues. That was a time in Harlem where money was everywhere.

Anyone could go on "The Hill" (Washington Heights) and cop some weight from the Dominicans and become "hood rich" in no time. Back then, a kilo of cocaine was probably going for $16,000-$17,000, so one-eighth of that may cost around $2,000. If you started off small, like most of us did, with an ounce, it may cost you around $450.

You're probably wondering how much could be made off that. Let's see… An ounce is twenty-eight grams. Back then, using plastic vials to package the product, you could at least triple your money; maybe even quadruple it. Let's say triple it, for argument's sake. You spend $450 and after packaging, you end up with around $1350. You can do one of two things: you can reup (get more product) with your original investment of $450, or you can double the investment to increase your profit. A smart person would double it of course, going back to "The Hill", spending $900. Now you've got a profit of $450. This process would repeat itself until you reached a comfortable level of weight to supply your block's demand. The other option was to go for the gusto until you reached a whole kilo. Now, some of you may have read other hood novels and heard countless stories of people who were making significantly more money than that. I'm not disputing that was routinely done. I just know how it went down on my block. Remember, this was during a time when money flowed; you might have had to reup once or twice a day!

That's just how a portion of the drug traffic flowed. Let's do some more math: $900 profit multiplied by seven days a week. (Oh, there were no days off) If a mf wanted to get high, you was on the job. $6,300 multiplied by four weeks, leaves you at $25,200. When you multiply that by twelve months you have yourself $302,400. And

13

that's just your profit. You now find yourself running a crack business that's close to half a million dollars annually. Now I don't know about you, but that's a lot of money for a teenager to be making. Most of us made more money than our parents and I'm using modest estimates. This is an example of just one person's earning potential. There were a few of us doing the exact same thing on the block. There was enough to go around for everyone. Times were definitely good back then but as you've probably heard, with drugs comes violence following close behind.

Not everyone on the block was into the drug game; some chose a more treacherous path; the way of the gun. I neglected to say this in the beginning so I'm saying it now, by no means am I condoning or glorifying any illegal acts that I speak of. I'm often ashamed of the life I chose.

I spend a lot of time wishing I'd made better decisions, wondering how my life would've turned out. I know you've heard the expression "hindsight is 20/20." Unlike others who may not admit it, I have many regrets, too many to mention; that's another book in itself.

Anyway, Reg wasn't a hustler in the crack game. He tried many times to no avail; shit would always go wrong or he mismanaged his business. Either way, selling drugs just wasn't for him. Reg and a few others from the block chose the way of the gun. It's a decision I swear I wish they hadn't made. Had they chosen another path, I probably wouldn't be writing this, but what's done is done. Reg became what I would call, "The Quiet Assassin" or a "Clown Thug." He was always joking around, ready to pull a prank. Reg had a sense of congeniality about him that everyone was drawn to; I mean *everyone*. Just because a guy is quick with his gun, doesn't always mean he can't fight. Reg was that exception; he was nice with his hands and loved boxing. So much so, he convinced the whole block into forming a love for the sport. I credit my love for the "Sweet Science" to him to this day. There were times when we would go to the local boxing gym and spar to get our skills up. True to his character, Reg would make jokes about whoever took the most punishment that week. He was a clown but don't let his good nature fool you; he was a dangerous mf. If you had a problem with him, it was a serious situation!

If Reg wanted something you had, he was taking it. If you fucked with someone he loved, he was coming for your head, no ifs, ands, or mf'ing buts! But back to boxing: Reg competed in the Golden Gloves a few times but ultimately never went far. He never committed himself to training the way he should have, dedicating himself to his craft. Had he taken it more seriously, who knows how far he could've gone. Reg had aspirations of becoming a professional fighter one day but the allure of the street got hold of him and wouldn't let go. Sad to say, it was like that for a lot of us.

Eventually, with a young daughter to provide for, he did what was second nature for him and he picked up his gun. Reg's motto was, *"as long as I know where the money is, my kids won't ever go hungry,"* and he lived by that. Others from the block chose the same path, my cousin, Gee being one of them. (I'll speak more about him later.) Whenever Reg "could catch a lick," as he would say, he picked that gun up.

A Rolex here, a chain there, an occasional crack spot, or any nigga that was getting a couple of dollars was fair game. Reg once told me how he chased a popular rapper from Queens through an underground parking garage as the guy screamed for his life. I thought it was funny at the time, but then again, I had a sick sense of humor back then. That was how Reg made his living. It was a twisted, violent lifestyle; a path suited only for the audacious. This lifestyle was one where life and freedom were routinely placed on the line to provide for loved ones. A path Reg knew could cut his life short but he took that chance anyway. He dared to travel the path that would ultimately cost him his life at the tender age of thirty.

Leroy "Big Lee" Phinazee
1969-2002

On the other side of gunplay was a smoother, mellow path that required more patience and finesse when compared to the instant gratification of a stickup. It took more of a business mindset; the corporate skills of a young entrepreneur, like those of a company exec.

Lee had such a mind for business. He turned a small crack operation into a tremendously successful enterprise. He recruited guys from the block and they happily profited as well. Dividing the work into three shifts, he made money sixteen hours a day. Lee grabbed his slice of the pie and never let go. His empire was built in the park on Lenox, or as it's more infamously known, The Danger Zone. At the time, it was wide open, primed for drug traffic, and the traffic was certainly there.

Lee's flow was one you couldn't help but notice. There were times when a $500 pack of nickels (containing $5 bottles of crack) came out of the building and was gone in less than two minutes. One person took the money while another passed out the work. That's one hundred bottles of crack sold in no time. I witnessed this with my own eyes time and time again. Unbelievable, right? That was a normal occurrence back then. Wherever Lee got his work from, it was A-1 quality.

His crew was in place and his flow was off the hook; what more could a young man ask for? What more could he want? For Lee, it wasn't enough; he wanted more. He wasn't content with the money he was making, even though it more than provided for those he loved. Lee didn't want anyone else to have the same success he'd achieved. If he lived in the penthouse, you couldn't live on the same

17

floor. Shit, that nigga didn't even want you in the same *building* as him! Remember, growing up, Lee and his brothers always had more than the rest of us on the block, and that set him apart. He placed himself on a pedestal, where in his mind, he reigned supreme. If someone even attempted to reach his level, it was perceived as a threat and he responded accordingly. Lee couldn't help himself. It was as if no one was supposed to have nice shit but him.

Money wasn't the only thing he craved; Lee also had a thirst for superiority. He needed to be the center of attention. Lee was the alpha male who always had to be in charge. He thought he should run the block and what he said, went. That was all there was to it. Notice I said he *thought* that way; that's not necessarily the way it always went. Don't get me wrong, he had a few that followed but most of the block did their own thing. His mistake was trying to lead with intimidation.

Standing over six feet tall, dark-skinned and handsome, the ladies found him to be easy on the eyes. But Lee chose to use his size and aggressive demeanor as a strategic tool in order to seem daunting. Like I said, it worked for some, but one particular person made this difficult for him and that was Reg. You see, Reg also had a very strong personality but he was the antithesis of Lee. People gravitated to Reg out of love and respect. He made everyone around him feel comfortable and accepted people for who they were. He had a genuine love for the block and everyone in it. While they sometimes bumped heads, Reg and Lee had a special bond of love and loyalty. The two of them were "as thick as thieves." Although on opposite sides of the game, they had each other's backs no matter what. Reg had a soft spot for Lee and the two of them formed a union no one thought would ever be broken, and for a long time it wasn't. But as the saying goes, "all good things must come to an end."

As years went by, Lee's lust for supremacy festered into a full blown envious mentality and this put a strain on their relationship. They would go through periods of distancing themselves from one another but those times were usually short lived as Lee would work his way back in Reg's good graces. Reg's personality wouldn't allow him to stay angry with Lee for long. There was more strength in unity than in division and both men realized that.

Lee's motives for keeping Reg close weren't always pure. He needed to align himself with a man of Reg's caliber at all times. Make no mistake, Lee wasn't soft by any means; he was no pushover but his demeanor and attitude deserved more credit than his actual deeds. The way he carried himself is what kept people away, not the work he put in. The fact that people knew he had the whole block behind him if necessary, especially, Reg worked in his favor. Not saying he needed to, but he would always call Reg when he had a situation. There were times when Lee would get into tiffs with outsiders and Reg would be right there, gun in tote by Lee's side, either squashing the beef or handling his business the way he saw fit. That was the thing about Reg; he was loved and respected by just about everyone. He was somewhat of a diplomat, or liaison for the block, so to speak. For this reason, 139th Street avoided a lot of conflict with other blocks, some of whom I will speak of later. This was another reason Lee felt slighted. He couldn't stand the fact that people embraced Reg and not him.

Needless to say, this back and forth love affair with those two went on for years. Lee's life would have its ups and downs, highs and lows, like everyone else's. One high was the birth of his first child, a daughter; and a low being two prison bids. Lee would eventually return home and rekindle his romance with the street, only this time with an exit plan in his crosshairs.

Lee's little brother was a young rapper who had the potential of being one of the biggest stars in the game. Parlayed the right way, their entire family would've benefitted from his talents, similar to a college player entering the draft. His little brother was that good! But Lee made poor decisions at times, like we all do. These decisions finally caught up with him; he'd rolled the dice one time too many. When you stay in the game too long, eventually you're going to ace (for all those who play Cee Lo). Lee played, so he had to pay. He paid the ultimate price. He paid with his life.

Lamont "Big L" Coleman

1974-1999

While most of us from 139th Street were either in the drug game or living by way of the gun, others traveled down yet a different path. Some played basketball and could've had promising careers. Others felt street life wasn't for them and went on to college or got jobs after high school. After all, everything is not for everyone. As young men, we made our way through life exploring the talents we discovered we had. In order to survive, you had to be half decent at whatever you chose to do. But every now and then you come across someone who had a special gift. Undefeated, multi-title holder, champion boxer Floyd Mayweather (my all-time favorite fighter) said other fighters were talented, but he was "God Gifted." Some may dispute this, but Big L was one who I believe fell into that category.

He was a young rapper whose lyrical prowess dominated over those who dared to challenge him. I personally witnessed him battle Jay-Z and I have to say, at the time, it could've been a tie. Some say L got him, others say Jay. I called it even. Anyone who knows me, knows that's big, because Jay-Z is my favorite rapper. Not saying he's the best of all time, but he's my favorite. Big L was able to hold his own back then up against a young Jay-Z and countless others. That should speak for itself. But wait, there's more.

Many of your favorite artists of today give L his props when it comes to the mic. On 50 Cent's "Patiently Waiting," Eminem, one of the most brilliant lyricists to ever spit, placed Big L on the same level as the Notorious BIG and Tupac Shakur, referring to the three as juggernauts of the rap game. Nas, when hearing Big L for the first time, said he was scared to death. He said, "Yo, it's no way I can compete if this is what I gotta compete with." Mac Miller credits Big

21

L as his early influence, saying it was L who inspired him to be clever and witty. He went on to say that in his early stage of rapping, he was trying to be Big L-trying to be a super raw MC. And there are many others who pay homage to Big L's skills. Need I say more? Big L was nice and I believe I speak for the masses when I say this. He even influenced others to explore their talents. Childhood friends Herb McGruff, Ma$e, and Cam'ron will undoubtedly say he motivated them to throw their hats into the rap ring. They all made their mark in the game, with Ma$e and Cam'ron attaining superstar status.

All the talent in the world, however great one may be, means nothing if it's bestowed upon someone who wastes it. Not saying this was the case with L, because he did what was necessary, using his gift to spark a career in music. But he had one foot in music and the other still stuck in the street.

Had he abandoned the negativity and focused on hip-hop, Big L could've been one the greatest MCs of all time. Sadly, we'll never know how far his music career would've gone. The underworld of drugs and street life is no place for someone who possesses the aptitude to take them out of the hood. This life consumes you. It will chew you up and spit you out with no regard for you, your family, or friends.

Once again, another man fell victim. He was one who had so much potential and promise; we all had high hopes for Big L. He was "The One." Just when his career was about to take a major turn for the better, he was struck down by the streets. If only he would've walked away completely, or more importantly, if he was allowed to. The influence of his older brother would eventually cost him and his family a lifetime of pain and sorrow. Dreams would no longer be fulfilled. His mother would lose a son. Hip-hop would lose a potential legend and the world would lose another black man to the streets.

Gerard "Gee Love" Woodley

1970-2016

This was probably the most difficult part of the book to write. At the time of this writing, the pain was still fresh from losing Gee. As I write this, he's been gone less than two months. Although the deaths of all four individuals hurt me tremendously, this one hurt the most. We were born as cousins but raised like brothers. Gee and I were actually closer than he was with his brother, TC. While the love was always there, they had a tense relationship.

Gee was a complicated guy. He could be very serious at times and yet very playful at others. He loved to crack jokes and make people laugh. I used to love hearing him tell a story; he was so emphatic and the way he described things was hilarious. Always conscious of his appearance, Gee stayed physically fit and did his best to keep up with the latest fashions. The only downside: he didn't always have the money to maintain his expensive taste.

Gee was no hustler. He didn't have the patience to take the time and learn the game. That nigga didn't even know how to use the scale. Selling drugs just wasn't his thing. Gee wasn't going to get a job or go to college and he didn't play ball, so his options were limited. The only thing left was the way of the gun, same as Reg. Choices, people. Nevertheless, that was his path.

Gee embarked on a trail of violence that would include armed robberies and other treacherous acts. It was a horrible way for Gee and Reg to make a living but it's the road they chose to travel. Between licks he would do his best to survive until the next come-up. His adult life had its ups and downs like everyone else's. He did a couple of stints on Rikers, a four year federal prison bid, and finally one in a New York State prison for five years, all while still on a paper chase.

Gee always maintained a lofty eye for a better life, but never quite achieved it. After his federal bid, he actually got a job as a maintenance worker, moved out of state and left the game alone for a while. Of course, he always had his ear to the ground for the occasional come-up, but kept his job in the meantime. I was proud of him. Gee was on the right path for a change; a path that would allow him to walk away unscathed and grow to be an old man. Leaving that life is a luxury many never get to enjoy, especially those who have lived a violent lifestyle.

Gee was on his way. But one thing most people do is make the mistake of returning to their roots. Gee used to frequent 139th Street because it was basically all he knew. The problem was, 139th Street is where he created lifelong enemies. No matter how much time had lapsed, he couldn't escape the stigma attached to his name. Gee did his best to navigate his past, shed that lifestyle and turn over a new leaf.

Sometimes the game won't allow you to walk away and escape your past. Some are not as fortunate to make it out as others. Like I said, people don't forget. After being home for only nine months from a five year state bid, the life finally caught up with him. Standing in front of his building one night, Gee paid the price for his past deeds. The cost was his life.

First Quarter

Where It All Began

What makes a person, man or woman, decide that in order to earn money they'll resort to criminal acts? There has to be some lack of sanity present when one makes such a choice, somehow rationalizing that the risk of committing a crime is outweighed by the reward one may receive. Notice, I said *may*. These are questions I never asked myself until having actually spent over twenty years in the street life. Was it worth it? It's definitely something to think about. I'll have an answer for you later.

There was a time when I didn't give a fuck about anything but making money in the street and I had a whole crew that felt exactly the same way. Although we did our thing separate from one another, we all had one common goal: to get as much money as we could and have fun doing it while at the same time, remaining loyal to one another and protecting the block at all costs. That was all that mattered. I mean, what else was there to care about? At the time, no one cared about the future. The motto was *"live now, worry later."*

It all started around 1986 or '87. Reg became cool with an older guy who was already in the drug game, named Marv. I'm not really sure how they met, but he hung around the neighborhood and they were cool with each other. Marv was really the one who introduced us to the crack game. I'd never even seen crack until 1987. He was hustling out of one of the abandoned buildings up the block toward 7th Ave. There was a demolished building creating a gap between two of the tenements where Marv hustled from. Customers would walk in the alley, stick their money through a hole in the wall and the worker would give them the product. Marv needed workers, so Reg put a couple of dudes down and so it began. He showed Reg the ropes and Reg started making money under his tutelage. Marv also introduced Reg to the connect (supplier). He was a Dominican up on The Hill by the name of Ernesto; we called him Ernie. His nose was big as fuck. That nigga shit looked like somebody put two tubas next to one another when you stared him square in the face.

Marv would take Reg up The Hill on 141st and Hamilton Place to Ernie's spot so they could become familiar with one another. That way, Reg could go reup whenever Marv was unable. Ernie was a super cool dude. Down the line, he would introduce us to his lawyer, Cabrera, for when the inevitable legal problems would arise. And did they come? You better believe it! Put it this way, Cabrera probably put at least one of his kids through school with the money that came from our block.

Things were going well for Reg, Marv and their crew for a while. But as always, the bullshit was never far away. Somehow Marv got into a situation with these three chicks that had access to a lot of weight. I don't know if it was over business or if he was romantically involved with one of them, but somehow the relationship soured. I can't say for sure, but I don't think it was about business because Marv was already getting his supply from Ernie.

Now of course, women with that much weight had to have reinforcements, so if a problem arose, backup was never far away. I think they were aligned with a strong crew from Queens. Whatever the problem was with Marv, it was enough to call for that backup.

At the end of every summer, the block association would hold our annual block party, usually right before the kids went back to school. Everyone loved the block parties. The music would be playing while kids rode their bikes up and down the street. You could smell the aroma of fresh barbecue as people tended to their grills. The ice cream truck would come to the corner by the police barricade and someone would pay a couple hundred dollars for all the kids to get whatever they wanted. The festivities went on all day and into the night.

The night of that particular block party, about a dozen guys all dressed in black jackets and long coats walked from 7th Ave down through the block party setting up on the Lenox Ave side of the park. Keep in mind, it was still summertime, so that shit didn't look right at all. Niggas peeped what was going on and went to get right.

We didn't know what was going on, but we definitely weren't going to sit there and find out empty-handed. TC went to the crib and got the pump shotgun, wrapping it in a plastic bag so it wouldn't alarm the older people in the block. TC crossed the street into the park and sat the pump under his legs, just waiting to see what these hooded niggas in black were up to. Reg joined him a few seconds later, along with Whitey.

As soon as he sat down, shots rang out. That shit sounded like fireworks on July 4th! With so many guns firing all at the same time, it made an unbelievable amount of noise. It was total chaos as people tripped, trying to run away and kids were crying and screaming. TC pulled the pump out and tried to fire but it jammed. Reg snatched the gun from TC's hands and tried to do the same with the same results. This back and forth with the shottie was going on while mfs were shooting at them. Having no luck with the firearm, TC took cover behind the big wall in the park, while Reg and Whitey ran toward the alley between buildings 100 and 104. At that moment, I saw Lee and Black Tone flying down the block, guns in hand, ready to handle their business.

Suddenly, just as quickly as the men had started firing, they stopped and disappeared out of the Lenox Ave/140th St side of the park. Once the smoke had cleared, everyone checked to see if anyone was hit. Fortunately, everyone was ok. Amazingly enough, no one had a scratch on them.

Later, we would find out that whole situation had to do with Marv. Point was well taken. They had come through the block looking for him but when they set up in the park and saw TC with the shottie, they just aired shit out. In the meantime, niggas in the block were furious! We didn't know where all this shit came from. When shit like this goes down, there's only one thing to do: homework.

Street investigations revealed that a guy (we'll call him "Country") was romantically involved with one of the three girls mentioned earlier. Country was Lee's cousin, but for some reason they weren't that close. To help you further understand Lee and Country's relationship, if Reg and Country had a beef, Lee would've rode with Reg on that, against his own blood. That showed not only how tight Lee and Reg were, but how much he didn't fuck with his cousin. It may not seem off to some, but it's still a little peculiar. Keep that in the back of your mind because it plays a part later.

Country hung out with niggas outside the block more than he fucked with us and it was cool. No one really thought about it too much because he had no real loyalty to the block; it was easy for him to side with the chicks and her people over us. It could've been out of love for her, or the chance to get down with a strong crew. In my opinion, if a person bases their loyalty on opportunity, they'll hitch their wagon to whatever train is doing well at the time. I call that the "Pachanga Effect."

Whatever his motive, that's the decision he made. The chicks knew Country was from 139th, so they figured he had to know Marv. They used Country to find out where Marv laid his head. Country knew who worked for Marv and figured that was the way to get close.

One night, Marv's worker and his girl went to his crib at the end of a shift. When the worker arrived, he was met by gunmen who forced him to take them right to Marv's door. As the worker knocked on the door, Marv recognized him through the peephole and opened it. The gunmen rushed in the apartment, letting the worker and his girl run from the building as fast as they could, feeling lucky to be alive. I don't have to say what happened next. When Reg got the news he was devastated. He lost a mentor and good friend; but when someone dies a violent death, all kinds of questions arise. Like who was the last person to see or talk to them? Who did they have beef with? These questions and more raced through everyone's minds. Reg was the closest to him so he had the more burning desire to get to the bottom of things; he needed to talk to the worker.

Immediately into the interrogation, the worker vehemently denied knowledge of the gunmen's identities. No matter how Reg pressed, the worker didn't crack. It now became a process of elimination. The streets talk and shit always comes together in the end. Somehow it got back to Reg that Country had some involvement because of the girl. That information put Reg hot on Country's trail. When Country got wind of this, he got missing with the quickness. Now I'm never one to take away from any man's capability to hold his own in the street, but let's be realistic. Some niggas are more brazen than others. You have guys that will kill someone in a New York minute; then you have some who are too afraid to defend themselves in a fistfight. I don't judge; I just call it like I see it. No matter where you may fall on the scale, from coward to killer, I believe every man deserves respect. *Everyone.* But niggas knew Country and he wasn't going up against someone of Reg's caliber, at least not alone. Niggas noticed how suspicious it looked when Country was avoiding the block more than usual. That mf wasn't trying to bump into Reg. But my thing is, if you have nothing to hide, why make yourself scarce all of a sudden? Country knew shit could get thick for him, so he reached out to niggas in the block.

Anyone born in the nineties and later may not identify with this, but back in the day there weren't many cell phones. Everyone used beepers and payphones. Phone booths were on almost every corner in NYC. They were everywhere! On the corner of 139th and Lenox Ave's uptown side was a payphone that Country used 24/7. He used it so much we used to call it his office. I guess Country got tired of ducking and somehow he got word to Reg that he wanted to meet by the phone on Lenox. He needed to check the temperature around the way. It was in its infancy, but Reg was becoming a dangerous mf and Country knew not to fuck with him. He also had the same feeling about Lee. When Country reached out, he specifically asked for Reg and TC to meet him at the payphone at a certain time. For his own reasons, he excluded Lee; why, I don't know. But this infuriated Lee, as he bit his bottom lip looking off to the side as he always did when he got angry.

Before they left for the meeting, TC and Reg strapped up. They had to be cautious when it came to Country because he had no real loyalty to niggas in the block. As the three of them discussed what was about to go down, Lee said the strangest shit. He said, "If that mf starts talking stupid, give it to him!" Reg and TC looked at him like he was crazy. They thought, *did this nigga just give us the green light to murder his cousin?? How could he say that about his own blood?* Good relationship or not, how could you feel that way about your own family? It might be crazy, but he said it.

32

When Reg and TC got to the corner, Country wasn't there. As they waited, the phone rang. Reg answered while TC was on the lookout for anything suspicious. Country was on the other end of the line. When Reg asked him why he called instead of coming through, Country said, "I'm not stupid. I knew y'all was gonna try to get at me." Reg assured him of his safety if he came and talked in person, but Country wasn't hearing any of it. He stated his piece over the phone.

At this point, Reg already felt Country was involved with what happened to Marv and he just wanted confirmation. Reg asked him about the worker and why he didn't get touched. Instead of saying he didn't know, Country slipped up and told Reg the worker and his girl were spared because of him. That was all the confirmation Reg needed. If Country was innocent, he wouldn't have been able to stop any harm intended for the worker and the girl. The gunmen didn't know them and had no reason to spare them. That means he was there or he spoke on their behalf.

Either way, his involvement was clearly evident. Reg knew what he had to do, but his hands were tied. There was no way of touching the three chicks or their crew because no one knew where to find them. Not long after, Country left the block for good and started life over somewhere else, so Reg ended up eating that loss. But he vowed, if Country ever came back to Harlem, he'd kill him. With Marv gone, the spot was left for Reg to take over. But this time he wanted TC and Lee with him.

They would eventually put another guy from 140th down, named Shake; the four of them took over where Marv left off. Reg introduced the crew to Ernie and he was cool with meeting them on the strength of Marv.

So began a budding alliance with Ernie and the new crew. Things were going well for the four of them. After a while, the arrangement between them needed to be altered. Reg and TC worked one week, Lee and Shake would have the next. I'll explain why that became necessary later. As their clientele grew, the more work they would get from Ernie. One eighth became two eighths, and two became three before anyone knew it. They were up to half a key (kilo), and so on.

Business was booming and it showed. Niggas stayed fresh with all the latest shit. You're probably wondering why I haven't spoken about what kind of cars niggas had. That's because we didn't have any. I can't front, we started late in the game compared to other blocks and we didn't really aspire to buy cars back then. Only a handful of us even knew how to drive. We were happy just catching cabs wherever we went. Other crews had whips though. They also had older niggas to look up to, show them the ropes, so to speak. The only one who was afforded that opportunity was Twin. He worked with some dudes from 140th that were getting major paper. All Reg had was Marv (RIP).

So while all the cars, jewelry and shit went on around us, we were just getting our beaks wet. Anyway, Ernie took a liking to the new crew. He treated them like extended family, showing them mad love. Ernie gave TC his first gun. It was a Smith and Wesson snub-nosed .357 Magnum. Reg's first was a nickel plated Taurus .38 revolver. Later, Reg would come to get his hands on a .45 automatic. I can't remember what brand, but that was his baby. That nigga loved that shit. As time went on, the block accumulated a wide variety of handguns, shotguns, rifles, Tech's, Mac's, AK's and any other shit we could get our hands on. The amount of firepower we had was ignorant; just dumb. Sometimes when I think back, I just shake my head. We were off the hook!

Reg, TC, Lee, and Shake were the breadwinners in the block at the time. Except for Twin, they were the only ones making any money back then. They made the money. They held the firearms. They had the power and they held the block down.

It was time to step shit up. After Marv got hit, the four moved their operation from behind the wall in the alley into one of the buildings where people were already hustling. A Jamaican crew had an apartment on the 2nd floor they worked out of. Reg and the crew moved in on the 2nd floor too, just down the hall. Back then, to distinguish one from the other, each crew would use a different color top, or cap. The top was used to seal the work inside of the vial, or bottle, like a wine cork. Once you established a color, you stuck with it. If you decided to change, you had to let the other crews know. It didn't matter, as long as no two crews had the same color at the same time. That would've created a huge problem. This color-coding system was put in place as a matter of respect and it helped build your clientele. If you had better product, customers would automatically ask for your color or go to your spot. At that time, everything was going as planned. But of course, life always throws curveballs; how you step up to the plate and swing your bat determines the measure of the man.

As time went on, Reg and TC noticed Ernie giving them less work than the time before as they went to reup. Back then, they were getting all their work on consignment, or credit. When Lee went to reup, if he was short on cash, he told Ernie that Reg and TC would bring the difference when they came. The problem with that was he never told TC and Reg. So when they went to reup, Ernie took whatever Lee owed off the top and gave them the difference, thereby lessening their work. Less work meant less profit. Less profit meant a serious f'n problem. That made them mad as hell. Now confronting Lee, he claimed he didn't understand it either. He just knew he was always coming up short when it was time to see Ernie. So now they had homework to do. They came to find out Shake was getting high, so of course money was going to be short. When Shake got to the spot, he would sit in there with the workers and get f'd up.

To solve that problem, they all agreed Shake couldn't bottle up the work or be in the spot anymore. He could check on shit, but that was it. Lee bottled up all the work from then on, and split the profit at the end of the package. Problem solved, right? Hell no! That seemed to work for a while but then the same bullshit happened again. When Reg and TC went to see Ernie, he gave them less work. '*Not this again*' they thought. What the fuck could be the issue now?! To their knowledge Shake wasn't allowed in the spot, or bottling up anymore, so what was the problem? When confronted, Lee's response would be, "Oh, I let Shake bottle up because I had something to do. Besides, that nigga had to do *something* for this money. Shit, he was getting paid for nothing!" That was Lee's logic. He assured them it wouldn't happen again because he wouldn't let Shake near the work anymore.

What's f'd up is that they wouldn't find out what the problem really was until later when a guy came to the block to give Lee some money. Lee wasn't around, but the guy knew they were all down together so when he saw Reg and TC he said, "Here's the money I have for y'all. I need another pack." They looked at him like he was crazy. TC asked him where he got the work from and he said, "Lee." Right then, they knew Lee was doing some back door shit.

You see, once he found out Shake was getting high, Lee saw that as a way to skim off the top without anyone knowing. He gave packs to someone outside the block, kept the money and blamed it on Shake's addiction. When confronted, Lee tried to say he was going to tell them about it later and that he only did it because he was trying to expand their business. It made sense, but wouldn't it have also made sense to tell his partners up front? I would think so. If his intentions were pure, why hide it? Of course, TC and Reg were furious. More than that, they were hurt. How could their brother steal from them? On top of that, he blamed it on Shake, who was considered a brother as well; tarnishing his name and making them look at him with the side eye.

All this was done because Lee wanted more for himself. Reg wanted to kill him. But how do you kill your brother over money? They loved Lee too much for that, so they let it slide. But now, Reg and TC had to come up with a solution of their own. That was the reason why the arrangement had to be altered. From then on, TC and Reg worked one week, Lee and Shake took the next. That way, each team would work and reup on their own. When it was Reg and TC's week, they would set $100 a day to the side each, for Lee and Shake, just to keep money in their pockets until it was their week, and vice versa. This system worked pretty well for a while. However, mismanagement of funds and niggas just being all over the place forced things to go further south.

It reached the point where Ernie wouldn't give anymore credit; everything was cash only. That worked for a short time, too. But of course, it didn't last. Between the four of them, they didn't have money to buy more work, and that was sad. They were some poor excuse for hustlers. When you're young and carefree with no guidance, what do you expect? Four different personalities, four young black men with pockets full of money and no one to show them the importance of saving or investing. It was the perfect storm. It's a wonder it lasted as long as it did; the whole situation was shameful. So where were they to go from there? No consignment and no money for reup. They ended up owing the connect thousands of dollars from back when they were still able to get credit. The only reason they were still alive was because of Reg. Ernie had a fondness for him that probably saved all four of their lives. They were alive, but still cut off. You know the expression "when it rains, it pours?" While trying to scrape up money to buy work, they would check on the spot periodically to make sure shit was intact.

One day, TC and Reg went into the building to do just that. When they got inside, there standing in the hallway was the biggest, blackest Jamaican they had ever seen. This mf was diverting customer traffic away from TC and Reg's spot. Looking back, it was probably out of frustration from being broke, but TC made a big deal out of it. He felt disrespected, so he told the man not to be in the building directing traffic. He said, "If the customers go to your spot, cool. But don't turn them away from ours! Even though we don't have work right now, don't do that shit!" As soon as he said that, the Jamaican pulled a big-ass gun out of his back waistband, cocked it, got within three inches of TC's face and started yelling so hard, the spit was flying, in a thick accent TC strained to understand. To this day, TC says he couldn't tell you what that mf said if you paid him a million dollars. With no gun on him, all TC could do was say, "Ok, you got it."

When they left the building, Reg, always clowning, asked TC "What's up? Whatchu gonna do?" All this is while laughing at him at the same time, by the way. TC was so mad he had tears in his eyes! Back then, Jamaicans were considered dangerous. Those mfs didn't give a fuck about shit and they hated black American men. They would kill a nigga over here and just go back to their mf'n country without a second thought. A lot of niggas were afraid of them, but not TC and Reg. They didn't give a fuck! TC felt disrespected. Now the guns had to come out.

Later, TC and Reg went back up the block with them hammers this time. The Jamaican was standing on the stoop smoking, not paying much attention to his surroundings. TC and Reg crept up and fired multiple shots in the direction of the Jamaican giant. Blaow! Blaow! Blaow! Blaow! Blaow! After the first few shots rang out, the startled man scrambled to get back in the building as TC and Reg pulled their triggers repeatedly, piercing his massive body and splintering the door, making them both look like Swiss cheese. The two of them thought, *we just started a war.*

In the street, it's difficult to beef with a mf or another crew when you don't have money. They didn't have any saved or coming in. Shit was really pouring down on them. TC and Reg laid low for a while until the heat blew over. In the meantime, Lee and Shake got their hands on some work and were back hustling in the spot. After the shooting with TC and Reg, the Jamaican crew left, but it wasn't long before they returned. I don't remember what the situation was, but somehow another problem arose with the Jamaicans in the building; maybe it was retaliation for the shooting. This time it was Lee and Shake who had to hold it down.

Whatever the situation was, Lee and Shake handled their mf'n business. I remember it being a cold winter night. I was watching TV when all of a sudden I heard the exchange of gunfire. I could tell it was a shootout because shots would fire, cease, and more would follow. I remember noticing they were different caliber guns by the distinct sound each one made. We lived on the first floor so it was quick access to the street. Stepping outside the door and looking up the block I saw it was Lee firing mad shots into the building with the Jamaicans trapped inside! Lee took cover behind parked cars as they fired multiple shots back at him from the building. That shit was like the OK Corral! After running out of ammo, Shake came limping down the block with a Tech saying, "I got him! I got one of those mfs!" By this time, TC and Gee had come outside too. Shake Told TC to give him the pump; niggas kept most of the guns at our crib because our apartment was on the first floor and located right across the street from the park where everyone hung out. That made shit easily accessible if shit got thick. All of this is going on while Lee is still shooting it out with the Jamaicans! Back to Shake; TC gave him the pump, but the mf didn't have any shells in it! Shake limped all the way up the block with an empty shottie.

Niggas told jokes about it later, but at the time, it was no laughing matter! If you're wondering why Shake was limping, it's because weeks prior, he got himself arrested, ran out of the 32nd precinct and was hit by a cab. His leg was fucked up but that didn't stop him from handling his business when the time came. Shake was off the hook!

You're also probably wondering how all this took place in the middle of the street like it did, but back then there were fewer police on the streets and their response time was much longer than it is now. Niggas were able to get away with more shit before the cops showed up back then; when cops heard shots in the hood they hesitated to respond. Those mfs weren't trying to play superheroes; and they really didn't give a fuck if we killed each other. Nowadays, there are a lot more cops and since 9/11, cameras are everywhere, making it more difficult to maneuver.

A day or so after the smoke cleared, Lee and Shake got picked up and charged with attempted murder and weapons possession. Shake was ROR'd (released on his own recognizance) and the judge granted Lee a bail. Niggas thought Shake had snitched, but that wasn't the case. Lee had a prior arrest, and it was a violent charge. The Jamaicans basically vacated the premises and never returned. The shootout had all the older people in the block shook up. All of this shooting and carrying on wasn't going to be tolerated and everyone thought something had to be done. Lee's mother was the president of the block association and it was her own son doing the shooting. This didn't sit well with anyone. Lee and a couple of others attended the meeting with the block association to help smooth things out. It was at that meeting that the argument was made for the block to be protected from all outsiders.

No strange faces would be allowed to lurk on 139thSt. Our folks didn't have to worry about being mugged or robbed once they were in the block. We would act as sentries, so to speak. Once the block association was made comfortable, things went back to normal.

With the Jamaicans gone, things were left wide open for business up the block. There were still other people hustling out of the building, but they never presented a problem so the crew allowed them to stay. The only problem was getting work, so things were not all good just yet. When your back is against the wall you either fold or come out fighting. These niggas came out shooting; and this was around the time Reg and TC started doing stickups.

41

Lee and Shake got their hands on some work and started hustling again, but it was never the same. With Shake still feeding his habit, he was becoming more unreliable by the day. So whenever Reg and TC came across a lick, Lee wanted in. He didn't need to, but he wanted to. So be it. Because of the loyalty and love they had for Lee, they let him in. Now they were playing a very different game. This game separated the men from the boys. It's the exact opposite of selling drugs. There's no sitting back waiting for customers to bring the money to you. You had to go get it. You had to take it!

Having a couple of shootouts under their belts gave them the confidence they needed in order to delve into that territory and I guess they were ready. Although Lee, TC, and Reg were tight, Lee was also close with another homie from the block named Black Tony, or Tone. There were two Tony's on our block, Black Tone and White Tone, or Whitey. Their skin complexion spoke for itself.

Back in the day, Lee and Black Tone were really close; they were like brothers. When Lee was younger he had a very big heart. He was generous with the people close to him, and Black Tone happened to be one of them. Like I mentioned earlier, Lee's mom hustled, so she kept her sons fresh and they always had money in their pockets; more than most of us did as kids. Being so close to Black Tone, Lee would treat him to the movies, buy food and make sure Tone was alright whenever they were together. Lee was just an all-around kindhearted guy; that was how he was back then. He was super cool when he wanted to be.

Fast forward to when things weren't going so well for Lee. Black Tone was now getting money around the corner in Gus's Bar. This was a cocaine paradise. There about five or six people selling coke in the bar and they were all getting money. I mean, serious money. Gus's Bar was a gold mine and Black Tone had his slice of the pie selling dimes ($10) and twenties of coke to a predominantly working-class clientele. The tables had turned, so to speak. So when Lee was f'd up, he could always go to Black Tone to borrow a little something to get on his feet again. It was only right. Lee had been there so many times for him in the past and Tone didn't forget it. It was mutual love and respect. That's the brotherhood I wrote about earlier; and this is how Lee would stay afloat when shit got rocky for him.

Meanwhile, Reg and TC went on a mini crime spree. Their first job was a dangerous one; they robbed one of Cheese's workers. Cheese was an older guy who had several crack spots in Harlem. He was well respected and somewhat revered on the street. Cheese was close with another guy from downtown named Big Red, who had ties with The Nation of Islam. These were two powerful men back then and not too many people crossed them, at least not to my knowledge. Having said all of that, Reg and TC didn't give a fuck about none of that shit. Their ribs were touching and they wanted to eat, so they did.

Wearing masks, and each carrying a Tech 9, they crept up on an unsuspecting man who was half asleep in a chair on the 2nd floor of the building. Teetering on the hind legs of his chair with his back against the wall, he was sound asleep. Reg yanked on the front legs of the chair, causing him and the chair to hit the floor with a loud bang. The man opened his eyes to two semi-automatics staring him dead in the face. That's a hell of a night! After working all night, being dead tired, to then get robbed of everything you made. On top of that you have to explain all of this to your boss, who happens to be Cheese. Reg and TC made him give up the whole shift's earnings. They moved after midnight because most money was made during the four-to-twelve shift back then. The two of them probably split anywhere from $2,500 to $3,000 their first time out; not bad for a few minutes work.

Reg and TC felt they were on to something; so of course, the next night they were out on the prowl again and this time Lee joined them. But they couldn't hit the same spot twice, even if they wanted to. Cheese was no dummy. He locked his worker in a vacant apartment for a whole shift and fed him Chinese food when he got hungry. Cheese thought, "Fuck that! You won't get me twice!" But that didn't deter those three. They went to other blocks and stuck spots up, equipped with masks, Techs, black gloves, the whole nine yards. They were off to the races.

From 133rd to 145th, no spot was safe. At some point they decided to stop taking from the streets and focused on bigger things. The money they were taking from the spots was small compared to what they could've been getting, especially with the risks they were taking. All it took was for one of the spots to be strapped and ready, and they would've found themselves in another shootout, or worse. But now they needed a plan. What could they hit that was holding some real bread; that could possibly put them back on their feet? A bank. But before hitting a bank, they'd need experience controlling a crowded situation.

They needed practice and what better place then Gus's Bar? The only thing was, they knew the people who hustled there and didn't want to rob them; they only wanted the bar's money. Having Black Tone on the inside was an advantage; he could be their eyes and ears. He informed the three that the best time to hit was late Friday or Saturday night when most people hung out and spent their paychecks drinking and socializing. The booty would be fat around that time. By then, the barmaid should have four or five cash boxes put away and that should be enough to get them ready for the next big score. Although Black Tone wasn't getting a cut from the take, he was the inside man they needed for intel. On his signal, they were supposed to run in the bar and lay it down, make the barmaid empty the cashboxes and get the fuck out. Simple plan, right? Well, this is how it went.

Tone did let them know when it was ok to come through, but at the last minute, they recruited another dude who had more experience with this type of shit. Let's call him Lime. Lime was one of the most thorough dudes you ever met. Super cool and down for whatever! He heard about some of the capers Reg, Lee, and TC were pulling and he wanted in. The three of them trusted Lime and let him in on the jux. The only thing about Lime was he was super hyped, like on 1,000! This nigga could be in the middle of telling a story and get so amped, he might do a back flip. So this is what you were dealing with when it came to Lime. Anyway, back to the bar.

TC, Reg, Lee, and Lime were on the corner of 139th. The plan was to wait for the next person to exit the bar so they could catch the door (you had to be buzzed in), push them back inside and handle their business. But Lime was so impatient and hyped, he ran before everyone was ready! This nigga made it to the bar before they had a chance to pull their masks down and glove up. Lime was behind the bar with the gun in his hand high in the air. People were stunned. Everybody froze. TC pulled his mask down, ran to the bar door and knocked on the glass. Lime came from behind the bar and opened the door for the other three to get in. Once they were all inside, people knew shit was serious. They didn't have to do much because everyone complied. TC still yelled, "Get the fuck down!!!" Mf's dove to the floor face first like they were at Central Park Pool.

On each side of the bar were the restrooms, where hustlers took their customers to make coke sales, just to put some shade on the nightly activities; you didn't want to do shit out in the open. Someone came out of the bathroom only to be greeted with Lee's 9mm. He politely stepped back in, closed the door and locked the mf! It didn't matter. They weren't there for the patrons' money, only what belonged to the bar. Lime went back behind the bar, stuck the gun in the barmaid's face and made her give up the cash in the boxes. As he's doing this the other three are controlling the room, pretty securely, I might add.

When Lime was done, he ran out of the bar to the rendezvous point. The others followed soon after, backing out of the bar nice and easy; the jux was done. No injuries, and most important, no casualties. The job was a success. Now it was time to count the spoils. When they all met up, the money was divided, everyone taking their cut, hugging it out and making their way home to their families.

The next day, Black Tone informed the crew that they didn't get as much bread as they could have. Lime was so hyped, he'd left two cashboxes behind and they happened to contain the most money. But you can't get everything, every time. So that was a learning experience. Now they knew how to control a crowd in the midst of a robbery. Another notch was added to their belts. Now what?

They had some homework and planning to do. While deciding what the next job would be, a situation fell into their laps. An old timer named Nate had a few after-hours spots and social clubs in the hood. In these establishments, there were poker machines and bootleg liquor, so it was nearly a cash cow. One of the spots was on 137th St between Lenox and 5th Aves. This was the one they decided to hit. Once again, it was Reg, Lee, Lime, and TC. They waited until late to move to increase the chance for more cash. Masked up, gloved up, and of course armed, they made their way onto Lenox around to 137th St. This time, they'd have help from a lookout named Sonny. He wasn't part of the jux but they would definitely hit him off with something after the job was done.

When the four of them got there, Lime kicked the door in! Boom! Once inside, he found two ladies inside counting a shitload of money and he scared them to death. Reg, Lee, and TC came inside and locked what was left of the door behind them. The spot was empty aside from the two women. Shiiit, this was going to be easier than the bar! Lee and Lime locked the ladies in a bathroom while Reg and TC went to work trying to break open the poker machines and cashboxes and instead of helping, Lee and Lime were stealing candy and liquor. Reg looked at those niggas like they were crazy! TC told Lime to put the guns and masks in a bag and stash them under a parked car, not needing them anymore. With the ladies locked in the bathroom, they wouldn't cause any problems. Sonny was looking out anyway, so the guns would be safe. Lime goes outside and starts talking shit with Sonny about how much money is in the spot, and in typical Lime fashion, he gets hyped.

Going back inside, a few more machines are cracked and the phone rings. Everyone froze, looking at each other. What they should've done was let one of the ladies out to answer it, but they didn't. They broke all the machines and cashboxes open and started stuffing the bags with paper and change. Those bags were heavy as fuck! They were determined to get everything out of there. They weren't leaving anything behind this time. As they were getting everything together, the phone rang again. This *really* made them nervous but *fuck it*; they thought; they were ready to leave anyway.

As they made their way to the door, they heard a loud knock. You know, the authoritative kind that sends chills up any criminal's spine. Lee looked through the peephole, saw two cops at the door and started jumping up and down like his boots were on fire. TC whispered, "Who the fuck is it?"

"It's the cops," Lee whispered excitedly.

Shit, they all thought. *What's the plan? What's the plan?* Thinking on his feet, TC opened the bathroom door with a finger over his lips urging the women to remain silent. He told them the police were outside and they were going to open the door. He instructed them to tell the police some other men had tried to rob the spot, they saw them run out and came in to help the women. That was the best TC could do on such short notice and he thought it was a good idea because the guns and masks were stashed outside anyway. Little did TC know, Lime got so excited in the conversation he had with Sonny, he brought the bag of incriminating evidence back in the spot. I swear, if they didn't tell me this shit out of their own mouths, I would've never believed it. I could not make this shit up! Needless to say, that was a terrible idea. But at the time, TC didn't know. The women were shaken up, but they agreed.

Thinking everything was cool, TC told Lee to let the police in. As soon as Lee opened the door and the women saw the police they yelled, "It was them! It was them! They robbed us!" So in true NYPD form, they immediately drew their guns and made everyone, including the women, get on the floor as they called for backup. Upon searching everyone and the spot, they found the bag of guns and masks. TC looked at Lime like he had shit in his mouth. "How the fuck did you bring that bag back in here," he thought.

48

Officers slapped the cuffs on the three of them while another officer was examining the hardware he found in the bag. He noticed one of the guns was loaded with Black Talon bullets; they were designed to pierce right through police-issued body armor. And so the beating began. "You have cop killers!" That's what the media was calling them back then. Another one of the officers had to stop him from punching and kicking the three of them as they lied on the ground cuffed and defenseless. Notice I said "three of them."

At the time, Reg weighed about 120lbs soaking wet with two rocks in his pockets. Somehow, before the police came in, he managed to squeeze behind one of the poker machines where no one saw his little ass. The women were too shaken to even realize he was missing. Unfortunately for Reg, their memory soon returned as one of them pointed out that there had been four assailants. Lee protested, insisting she was mistaken. So the cops put TC, Lime, and Lee in the squad cars and searched the spot again for Reg. About ten minutes later you could hear Reg yelling, "Ahh! Ahh! Alright! I'm coming out!" Reg was getting the shit beat out of him with one of those heavy-ass black flashlights the cops used to have.

Now they had all four perps in custody. Off to the 32nd precinct they go, or so the guys thought. Instead, they were taken to a special robbery unit and interrogated for a full twenty-four hours. No food, no phone calls, nothing. The four of them were placed in multiple lineups before seeing a judge two days later. Cabrera, the attorney Ernie had put us on to represented Lee, but he spoke on behalf of all four of them at arraignment. The public defenders didn't have to say much of anything. Cabrera wanted to show the judge how the defendants had strong family ties in the community, so he asked everyone who was present for support to stand. The entire courtroom was on their feet. It was filled to capacity with everyone from the block; old, young, mothers, fathers, sisters, brothers, cousins, girlfriends, baby mamas, you name it. I don't know how, but it worked. The judge ROR'd them! He probably thought there would be a riot if he didn't.

Lee, Reg, and TC were released, but they had to leave Lime behind. He was on parole, so they gave him a bail and remanded him. The three were now back out on the street, but with an open case for armed robbery hanging over their heads. Now what?

Out on the street, with no income and families to care for and babies to feed. What's a man to do? They needed to make something happen. It's a good thing they had their parents to support them during this trying time. While waiting for their next court date, they were approached by a local numbers runner named Clarence, who was cool with Nate and knew about the situation. Clarence told them he would put a good word in with Nate on their behalf, and it worked. Clarence assured them Nate wouldn't press charges if they agreed to do some dirty work for him. That was music to their ears! Of course they would comply, and they thought forging an alliance with a man like Nate may have been a way to earn money in the future. This could work out for all parties concerned.

At this point, their minds were at ease. It took some of the pressure off those young shoulders. At their next court date, they saw Nate down at 100 Centre Street bright and early, ready to inform the DA about dropping the charges. *Damn,* they thought. *This could really work out for us.* But instead of withdrawing the charges, he told the DA that Lee, Reg, and TC threatened him, he was in fear for his life, and he couldn't walk the streets of Harlem knowing they were free. The judge bought that bullshit and remanded them for threatening and witness tampering. Niggas mouths dropped! This old sucka-ass nigga went all the way downtown to do some creep shit!

As Lee would say, "Ain't that about a bitch?" Now the three of them were off to Rikers. Back then, The Island was rough. It is now too, but there was a much different breed of prisoner back then from what you see now. For instance, if someone was a snitch, he had to sign himself into PC (protective custody); he couldn't live in population. Now, a mf will walk up to a CO and snitch in front of the whole house and nothing happens to him. So they were on the Rock for the first time in their young criminal careers.

I can't speak for certain, but I know they had to be a little shook. It's only natural, when someone is placed in an unknown environment; especially one as volatile and dangerous as that. But they handled themselves well. While on Rikers, their families had the task of getting bail money together. Of course, Lee was able to get out first. Back then, you didn't have to provide your source of funds, so an inmate could get bailed out by anyone, no questions asked. Lee's mother got him out as quickly as possible. Reg was next, and TC was last. That's because, quite frankly, we didn't have the money.

TC didn't want to have to go to who he knew had the money, our grandfather. He was ashamed of his actions and didn't want our grandparents to know. So, while sitting there, his girl at the time did the unthinkable. She stood outside with me and sold crack to get her man out of jail. I'm not going to lie, I was amazed by her actions. She was a trooper. Even more unbelievable to me, was that she was from Esplanade Gardens. Now, I don't want anyone to feel slighted, but although they're still in Harlem, places like Esplanade Gardens, Riverbend, Lenox Terrace, and Riverton were a little different from where we lived. It was more expensive to live in those complexes and the residents consisted of doctors, lawyers, and other professionals who were able to provide a more affluent life for their families. It's also where a lot of hustlers from Harlem moved, if they decided not to relocate to Riverdale, Yonkers, or Bergen County, NJ. Shit, Diddy was from Esplanade! So the kids that didn't attend private school may have gone to the same schools as us, but for the most part, you never saw them in the hood because they hung out in their perspective complexes. Their parents did their best to shield them from the streets we lived on, and with just cause. But of course there were always exceptions. The *guys* didn't really fuck with niggas like us, so for a chick from EG to actually come on the block and sell drugs was astonishing. I definitely tipped my hat to her. Niggas need chicks like that, especially if they're in the streets. But his girl didn't have to sling for long.

TC's mother informed her dad about the situation and he bailed TC out. Now the three were back on the street together again. After going back and forth to court for a while they finally took pleas and waited to be sentenced. TC, Lee, and Reg copped to a one-and-a-half to four-and-a-half year sentence. Lime received four-and-a-half to nine because he had prior convictions and was still on parole at the time of the instant offense.

Reg, TC, and Lee were scheduled to be sentenced on Nov. 16, 1989. For some reason, I'll never forget that date. They now had the whole summer out to get their affairs in order before starting their bids.

Lee started hustling in the building again while TC decided to explore new territory; he started hustling in the park. No one really did that before, being it was so wide open; there wasn't much shade you could put on your dealings. Drug transactions went on behind closed doors for the most part. Moving out on the street was frowned upon for safety reasons. You also wanted to shield your business from the old people and children. But, desperate times called for desperate measures. So TC made it work somehow.

Reg, on the other hand, just chilled. He wasn't really doing anything for money at that time. He would get bread from Lee, TC, or Black Tone when he needed. But that was it, really. Having the entire summer out, TC went extra hard to get his bread up. He started with twenty-eight grams and built that shit up to 125 grams in no time. 125 turned into 250, and so on. TC turned that shit all the way up! That nigga had the park rocking! He was working with a guy from 140th named Aziz.

After a while, I got down, too. It was the summer of '89 and it was one of the best summers I'd ever had. Money was flowing like water. Niggas had crazy fun! That year, Spike Lee's "Do The Right Thing" was in theaters along with the first "Batman" movie, starring Michael Keaton and Jack Nicholson. The hottest song that summer was 'Back To Life' by Soul ll Soul. There was something about how that break beat dropped that made even the hardest gangsta want to dance. Almost every car with a booming system pumped that shit as they cruised through Harlem's streets. You had to hear that song at least twenty times a day! That shit was crazy!

I used to walk around with a band in each pocket of my Gap sweatpants and some Reebok Classics on my feet. That's $2,000 in my pockets every day for no fucking reason. I know, I was ignorant as shit back in the day. Then, I got on some Nautica shit, hard. At the time, they had a flagship store on 70th and Columbus Ave. I used to wake up every morning, make a stack, and take a cab down there to buy a new outfit. I might have grabbed something to eat from Jackson Hole on 84th and Columbus, then shoot back uptown, shower up and finish out the day. Of course, I had my Fila and Christian Dior shit going on as well, but it was mainly Nauti. That's just what I liked. And this shit happened almost every day that summer. TC was on some other shit. He fucked with Nautica a little, but not like I did. But that's enough about me.

Things were going smoothly. When Lee saw the flow TC had generating down in the park, he wanted in. It didn't matter that he still had the spot up the block all to himself. Remember, we're all from the block, but Lee made it clear he wanted that all to himself. No one beefed. That's what Lee wanted, that's what Lee got. It wasn't because niggas were afraid of him; not everyone was. A lot of shit was overlooked because of the love niggas had for one another back then.

It's like this: everyone has that one person, or even a whole side of their family that acts like a f'n asshole. But there's nothing you can do. You don't want to be fighting them all the time and you definitely can't kill them (although you may want to). So what do you do? Just maneuver around their dumbass to keep the peace. Besides, TC wasn't a selfish, greedy person, so when Lee came to him and explained how shit wasn't going so well for him up the block, TC said, "Fuck it. Let's do it." His rationale was, 'I want for my brother what I want for myself.' That's the way TC always felt. These niggas were in the trenches together, so why not help if he could? So Lee came out with green tops while TC already had red. Now the traffic from up the block was being directed to the park along with the flow TC had already established. It was a win-win situation. All this is going while Reg is just sitting back, chilling. This was around the time when he and Gee really became close.

Gee was never a hustler so he basically stayed with Reg and followed his lead. This lasted all summer and into the fall when it was time for the three to turn themselves in. November came quickly, and time definitely flew with all the fun they were having but it all came to an end on sentencing day. That was a sad time for everyone in the block.

The morning of sentencing, Reg, Lee, and TC made their way down to 100 Centre Street to begin the next chapter of their young lives. The courtroom was filled once again with friends and loved ones; this time to see them off. Tears fell and hugs were shared before they left to face judgment. The charges were read and they were asked if they understood what they plead guilty to, just as they had been when they originally took the DA's offer. Once the judge, DA, and attorneys were all in agreement, the defendants were asked if they had anything to say. All three declined; they were cuffed and led to the back of the courtroom through the door next to the judge's bench. Reg, TC, and Lee went to the Tombs (Municipal Detention Complex) for a few days and then to Rikers Island. From Rikers, Reg and TC went to Downstate CF for reception into the NYS prison system. Because Lee was under 21, he went to Elmira CF which was the NYS reception facility for adolescents. Back then, you stayed in reception for two to three weeks before being transferred to a traditional housing facility.

For Lee, his next stop was Mid-State. Reg and TC went to Oneida. Both prisons were located in the same hub in central New York. Doing a bid is rough but doing it with your brother/co-defendant made it a little easier. TC and Reg both got regular visits and packages from family. Remember TC's girl, who went so hard for him? She left him during the bid but I can't say it was all on her. Before TC left, he got caught slipping with a few chicks and she stayed with him anyway, through all the bullshit. Some people are just not built for doing time with a loved one and she was one of them. She didn't leave right away, though. The visits, phone calls and packages were there in the beginning, but faded after a while. TC was f'd up over it, but what could he do but press on? He still had family support and made the best of it. Still, there's nothing like having your lady by your side during a f'd up time like that.

Lee was in Mid-State doing his time and had all the support he needed as well. His mom, kid's mother and other family members held him down one hundred percent. Another thing that helps a bid go smoothly is having some future plans in place for when you make your exit. Having something to look forward to besides a release date, gave a prisoner hope. The three of them were given a light at the end of the tunnel.

Before going away they had the opportunity to align themselves with two of Harlem's elite, Richard 'Rich' Porter and Carlos "Flaco" Cruz. Somehow, Rich and Flaco heard good things about the three and came through the block to chop it up with them. They had a small chat at first but agreed to meet at the pool hall on 145th. At that meeting, Flaco and Rich expressed their admiration for the unity and loyalty Reg, Lee, and TC had for one another. They offered the three a chance to get some real money with them. Rich and Flaco planned to flood 139[th]Street with as much work as it could handle. *'Damn, where the fuck were these niggas before we picked up those damn guns?'* they thought. The three regretfully informed Rich and Flaco of the fact that they had to go away for a bid. Ok, no sweat. They assured the three of them the same offer would be on the table the minute they stepped out of the gate. That was music to their mf'n ears. Just think, if you had to do a stint in the pen but knew there was a golden opportunity waiting for you upon your return, wouldn't that make shit a little sweeter?

Back in those days, Rich and Flaco were the niggas to be next to. Oh, you can't forget about Kody Mason. And then there was Richard 'Fritz' Simmons, but he was on another level. From 1984 to

1990 Rich, Flaco, and Kody made Harlem their playground. They were the youngest, richest niggas in Harlem at the time. Don't get me wrong, there were others who preceded them and I give them their props. Those men made millions largely through heroin and cocaine.

Money that was made in the '60s and '70s made '80s money look like chump change but when you speak of the crack era in the '80s, you cannot have that conversation without the names Rich, Flaco, and Kody. You just can't! They were the major players of that time and they set the tone for the streets. The cars, jewelry, and flash they displayed had every young nigga in Harlem trying to emulate them. As teenagers, they were driving European cars most grownups couldn't afford back then. Can you imagine driving a top of the line vehicle purchased with your own money at eighteen years of age? And I don't mean dropping a $5,000 deposit and paying notes. No, these mf's bought the car from the dealer on the spot, paid for in its entirety. Back then, niggas didn't know about credit or have a need for it. Even today, if you're not a rapper or athlete, you're not buying cars with cash money. But they did.

Rich had a half dozen luxury vehicles parked in the garage on 132nd and 7th Ave. BMW, Porsche, Mercedes Benz, Saab, you name it, they drove it. They also set trends when it came to fashion. Kody wasn't really the flashy type but he kept a fly-ass whip. Rich was more of what niggas aspired to be; it was said he never wore the same outfit twice. I don't know how true that is, but I wouldn't dispute it because he stayed fresh.

Always immaculately dressed and clean cut, his meticulous style was duplicated throughout Harlem, right down to his haircut. He wore a one to the grain and so did most of the hood. I can't front, my first mink was navy blue with a white stripe across the chest and sleeves, along with a matching baseball cap. I got the idea from a picture I saw of him back in the day. His was black with two white stripes on the sleeve. I didn't want mine to look exactly like his but I definitely tried to emulate his style. Shit, back then even rappers looked up to and wanted to be like the hustlers. It was well known that LL Cool J was good friends with Flaco and was seen chilling with him uptown on several occasions. Nowadays, it's the opposite. Niggas watch videos and want to be what they see.

Flaco was a different animal altogether. He was the flashiest of them all. That nigga was on 1,000 at all times! I don't even think the nigga slept. His energy drink was probably 97 Octane. Flaco was a wild mf, always over the top with everything he did. The first time I ever saw him, he pulled up to the basketball game on 139th St with a yellow, blue, and white dirt bike and the Motocross jumpsuit to match. He rode up on the sidewalk, fucked with some chicks for a few, and then broke out, poppin' a wheelie up the block to 7th Ave. Flaco loved the chicks, maybe more than the money. But he was oh, so misogynistic! This nigga would video tape sessions of him f'n chicks then play the video at The Rooftop, a roller skating rink located on 155thStreet between 7th and 8th Ave for all of Harlem to see. A lot of times these were niggas' chicks who slid off and f'd Flaco behind their man's back and he would expose their ass on that Rooftop screen. But what did niggas do? Nothing. A lot of mfs were afraid of Flaco because they thought the nigga was crazy. Then there were those who were so happy to be getting money with him, they let a lot of his antics slide. You could fill an entire book on some the bullshit he put Harlem through.

Flaco was a madman, but niggas loved him. Now Kody was the most laid back of the three. He made his money from powder coke as opposed to the crack Rich f'd with. But don't get it twisted, Kody made plenty of money. He held his own with both Flaco and

Rich but you couldn't really tell unless you saw what he drove. Kody was always clean cut but he dressed ordinary for a guy touching the amount of paper that he was. He preferred a low-key image, if he had to have one at all. Kody left all that crazy shit for Flaco. He did enough flossing for the three of them. Kody always kept a mean whip, though. This was Harlem in the 80's for my generation. It was a beautiful time, indeed.

Reg, Lee, and TC couldn't wait for their bids to be over so they could get back to the street and link up with Rich and Flaco. But their hopes would be cut short early. On Jan. 4th, 1990, Rich's body was found near Orchard Beach in the Bronx. He was shot multiple times in the head and chest. The family was devastated. More so, because a month prior, his little brother William "Donnell" Porter was abducted on his way to school on Dec. 5th and held for ransom in the amount of $500,000.

At first, people believed Rich was killed while trying to negotiate his brother's release without the help of the police. It was later revealed that his long-time friend was the actual culprit behind the murder. Flaco claimed it was a dispute over money. Rich supposedly lied repeatedly about a situation and Flaco felt he couldn't be trusted any longer, so he ended his friendship with Rich by taking his life. An even sicker plot unraveled as it became known that a member of their own family was the mastermind behind the kidnapping of little Donnell. When Rich was killed, there was no one to pay the ransom. Therefore, there was no reason to keep poor Donnell alive. His innocence was stolen at twelve years old, betrayed by his own blood. I always say, 'Just because someone is related to you, it doesn't make them family'. That was a sad, sad situation. My condolences go out to the Porter family. No parent should have to bury a child, yet Mrs. Porter had to bury two. She lost both of her sons, and Harlem lost its native son as well.

Harlem was in mourning, just as Mrs. Porter. It was a somber time in our hood. In my opinion, it was never quite the same after that. When Lee, Reg, and TC heard the news, they were crushed. Their dreams were destroyed by the greed and deception of the friends and family of Rich Porter. May he and Donnell both rest in peace. There was nothing left for the three to do but persevere.

Second Quarter

Coming Home

Incarceration can take a toll on the human psyche. I don't care how well a person may have seemed to adjust, doing time in prison changes you. For some, it's very noticeable while others may display subtleties you have to look for. Some people can do time. Others let the time do them. Suffice to say, Reg, TC, and Lee made it through this period in their lives fairly, considering the circumstances. TC was transferred to Edgecombe, a work release facility located in Upper Manhattan. A few months later, Reg went to the parole board and was granted release from Mohawk CF.

Everyone on the block was happy for the return of Reg and TC and was anxiously anticipating Lee's homecoming. We couldn't wait for The Three to be reunited so the block could be whole again. The wait wasn't long; less than a year later, Lee was transferred to Lincoln, another work release facility located on 110th St and Central Park North. The block was elated about Lee's return but for some reason, he didn't share the same enthusiasm as the rest of us. Being separated from his friends for the first time in his life had caused a change in him. While the seed had been planted long before, it really manifested itself during and after his bid.

When Lee was just a young man, his mother had told him he didn't have any friends. She told him the people he hung out with and loved were his "homeboys," not friends, and definitely not worthy of a brother. I can't say for sure, but I would take an educated guess that his mom felt that way because Lee's father was murdered by his so-called "friends." This was the type of malice and contempt she instilled in her son's heart.

At first, this bothered Lee a lot because he had genuine love for the people he grew up with. But I guess seclusion from Reg, TC, and everyone else made him re-evaluate his relationships. It was so evident that when he returned, Lee addressed everyone as "homeboy." This nigga knew everybody's name but insisted on calling us that dumb shit. Niggas thought it was weird at first but brushed it off. But Black Tone was the one that knew the mentality behind that "homeboy" shit because he was there when Lee's mother first made that remark. I believe that ideology was the spark that lit the fire in Lee's transformation from being down for his people to being down for himself. Don't get me wrong, he didn't act like that 24/7, but it came out from time to time.

A new chapter was upon Reg, Lee, and TC. But how do you make the transition from prison to freedom and how smooth will that transition be? Parole in NYC wasn't as strict as it is now; not all PO's forced you to be employed. You basically had to stay drug fee and avoid being re-arrested. This left plenty of time on the clock for a parolee to get into mischief. You'd think that after being locked up, a person would do everything possible to avoid going back. Most people are gun-shy when they first step out the gate but that shit wears off quickly. Sometimes when you're incarcerated, it creates a burning desire to pick up where you left off. You might want to hit the streets a hundred miles an hour, at full speed, and that's exactly what happened with TC.

He made his way back into the drug game, and instead of resuming activity in the park where he had enjoyed so much success, he went back up the block, to where it all began. In their absence, strange faces were hustling out of the old building and out on the street as well. That shit was a free for all! When TC saw this, he was disappointed. No one was there to hold down what had been established before their departure. He decided to clean house; with Reg backing him, he announced that everyone who wasn't from

139thStreet would have to leave. After that, he made it clear to those who were from the block and had allowed the outsiders to come in and set up shop that *they* had to vacate as well.

Reg and TC weren't having that bullshit all over again. There was little to no resistance. What could anyone possibly say? Reg, TC, Lee, and Shake were the ones who'd shed blood for that building. Nobody could say shit! From that point forward, it was established that no one could get money in 139th if they weren't originally from there. The only way an outsider could come in is if he was with someone from the block, and even then, he had to meet everyone's approval.

So TC was back in business. Reg would get his hands on work somehow and filter it in with the supply TC already had. Remember, Reg was no hustler, so this arrangement worked well for them.

Then something fell into their laps; something that would change the game for a minute. Reg was the type of guy everyone loved, making friends everywhere he went. People gravitated to him like bees to honey. One of his people gave Reg a brick (kilo) of some high-quality coke. Other than on TV and movies, this was the first time either of them had ever seen a whole kilo. They had eighths, quarters, and halves but never a whole brick wrapped up like on the big screen. They were captivated, like two kids at a magic show. This really put a battery in their backs. TC, a marketing genius, remembered the success he had selling deuces ($2 bottles) back in '89, so he convinced Reg to do the unthinkable. These fools got the kilo cooked, broke the whole thing down and sold $1 bottles. That had never been done before. It definitely made niggas sit up and take notice, even getting the attention of surrounding crews. One in particular was a powerful hustler from 142nd St. named Fatboy; he was the brains behind a notorious crew called The Lynch Mob. Fatboy approached TC and Reg about the $1 bottles because he couldn't believe the rumors he was hearing; he had to get it straight from the horse's mouth. Fatboy wasn't aggressive with his approach; they were all cool with one another. Like I said, everyone had love for Reg, and TC and Fatboy were both compulsive gamblers, so they shared that common thread.

Later, Fatboy would give TC work every now and then, if needed. The $1 bottle campaign was a success and TC and Reg were doing well for themselves. While all this is going on, Lee was re-entering society and decided to open up shop in the park again, recalling the success he and TC had enjoyed before they left. This time would be different.

The numbers he pulled in '89 paled in comparison to what he was able to do this time around. I'm talking, astronomical. Everyone was eating; it was all good. But remember how Lee asked TC if he could get money down in the park in '89? There was none of that this time. No one could hustle in the park or in its vicinity. Lee didn't give a fuck if you were from the block or not; the park was his and he wasn't sharing it with anyone; that's just the way he felt. Reg and TC had their own thing going on, so they could care less. All was good on 139th. The Three were home. Everyone was making money. Everyone was getting along. Times were good.

139th Street Gets a Name

While The Three had been locked up, local crews like The Best Out, Same Gang, CMB (Cash Money Brothers), Final 4, Slick & the Family, and All-Star were having a lot of success throwing parties, cookouts, and bus rides. Niggas would call home and hear about how dope the parties were and how much fun people were having. Niggas from my block didn't party much back then and we weren't very social, especially Lee, Reg, and TC; but there was something very alluring about that party life and they wanted to experience it. But how could they fit in with all those other crews? They weren't the same type of niggas. Reg, Lee, and TC didn't drink, dance, smoke weed, or any of that social shit. We didn't even have a name. Everyone just called us "139th St. Niggas." If we were to take a name, it had to be one that represented us without sounding too soft.

TC thought about their brotherhood. He took into consideration all they'd been through and how they'd come out shining through it all. Our bond was impenetrable and it was important to let the world know that our loyalty, strength, and unity was unwavering. We were young, black, strong, and well-respected in our hood. The name had to exemplify those qualities. No amount of money or outside entity would ever come between us. We were brothers forever. These were my brothers, my niggas forever, for life. Niggaz for Life. NFL. That was it. That was how we became known as The Niggaz for Life Crew.

TC was the first to represent by purchasing a blue windbreaker with the letters "NFL" embroidered on the chest and a turtleneck with the same on the collar. Reg and Lee quickly followed suit, and from that, NFL was born.

There was still the matter of fitting in with all the other crews around Harlem; those dudes were all getting money, partying and having a ball back then. Remember, niggas weren't all that social. What they decided to do was throw a basketball game in the park in honor of people from the block that had passed away, and what better time than Memorial Day weekend, the unofficial beginning of summer?

We asked The Best Out if they would play in the game. They agreed, but only on one condition: they didn't want to be called The Best Out because all of their official players wouldn't be available on that day and they didn't want to risk receiving an "L" (loss) on their record. It was understandable, so the flier read:

The One 4 One Crew v. The 139th Street NFL Crew

1st Annual Memorial Basketball Game

We didn't even have laminated fliers; our shit was on regular paper and we didn't care. We made hundreds of copies and walked all over Harlem passing them out like a record label street team. We walked all the way down Lenox to 110th St., over to the Eastside and back up to 139th. Some of us walked all the way to 155th in the Polo Grounds and Colonial Projects handing them out in hopes that people would show up. We had never done anything like this before but it was a success.

On game day, the park was filled to capacity; men, women and children packed the park to see the game. It was a proud moment for us. I won't lie; I didn't expect that many people to show up, but they did, and we were pumped. The "One 4 One Crew" wore black shirts with white letters. We wore aqua blue with white letters and matching Air Force 1's that read:

139th Street Niggaz for Life Crew

There's an infamous picture floating around on the internet and social media of us that we took after the game. That shit brings back so many memories. I can't help but feel nostalgic just thinking about it. I believe the legendary Luv Bug Starski was on the wheels of steel keeping the crowd entertained during timeouts and intermission. We also had somewhat of a ringer on our squad; a young college-bound prospect wanted to play for us so we gave him a shirt. He was nice with that rock! He was the son of a major player in the drug game who'd been locked up back in the day. When the kid was little, he used to come around on his bike and run errands for us, like riding down to 132nd and Lenox to McD's to get food while we hustled on the block. Once, his mom actually came out and thanked us for giving him money and keeping him out of the street life. I remember him bringing a duffle bag full of letters from universities all over the country trying to recruit him for their basketball programs; we were all so proud of him. Ultimately, he would go on to attend Georgia Tech with Stephon Marbury.

When he asked to play in the game that day, we said, "fuck it, he's like one of us." It was an advantage because he was nice, but a disadvantage because he was so young. Either way, we took it and he not only showed up, but he showed out! My man Steve Jordan was calling the game on the mic so every time he got the ball, I'd asked Steve to call him "Tha Youngsta." Even though we had "Tha Youngsta" on our squad, the game still ended up coming down to the wire.

The competition was tight as hell. With the clock having only seconds left, the ref made a bad call in favor of "The One 4 One."

Why'd he do that? One of our players knocked the ref out! He hit him so hard, the mf fell twice. The crowd went crazy and ran onto the court, basically ending the game. We don't know who would've won, but we were up by a point or two when the bullshit occurred so we just took the "W" (win) and ran with it. Fuck it!

After the game, there was a party in the park; music was playing, people were dancing, and celebrating the victory with us. Everyone was having a great time; it was a beautiful thing. But that night, things would take a tragic turn for the worst.

With the festivities lasting well after dark, people were still in the park enjoying themselves when a guy from 138[th]Street pulled out a gun, letting shots off in the air. Reg's cousin was there and he stepped to the guy because he knew him. He was known to us all but Reg's cousin knew him a little better because he was from 138th as well. He asked the guy why he'd do that dumb shit with all the kids and women around. Words were exchanged and they ended up fighting. Reg's cousin got the best of the guy and after it was over, he got on his bike and rode away. Niggas didn't think anything of it because it was a fair fight; one winner, one loser. That's that. Right? Nah.

The guy waited until Reg's cousin was away from the block, crept up and started firing at Reg's cousin, hitting him all in his side. TC, Reg, and the others were standing on our corner when they heard the shots a few blocks away so there was no real cause for alarm, or so they thought. A few minutes later, the same guy came storming past them on Lenox with that dangerous look in his eyes; you know, the way a mf looks after they just did some bullshit. So Reg asked him if he was good. Dude said "yeah" and kept it moving. So niggas brushed it off and resumed their conversation.

Reg later got the call that would change his life forever. Sad to say, his cousin perished that night. Devastation is an understatement; Reg took the news extremely hard. This pain was different from losing Marv. This was his family. It was a tough pill to swallow, indeed. This incident awakened a beast within Reg he probably didn't even know existed. The desire for revenge burned deep. Reg had to wait for the perfect opportunity to exact retribution but the wait wouldn't be long.

For a few weeks, he watched the dude drive around the hood like shit was all good. The mf came through 139th and everything, like shit was sweet. The sight of him drove Reg insane. One summer night, the guy and his cousin were in his ride. They drove up 139th and sat in the drive-thru at Wendy's. When Reg peeps it, he tells Gee to get his hammer. The line in the drive-thru was long so dude had been sitting for a minute; this gave Reg and Gee enough time to creep up the block. When they turned the corner, Reg snuck around to the driver's side of the car as Gee stayed on the passenger side. As the dude realized Reg had appeared out of nowhere, he tried reaching into the back seat.

Later, it was discovered that his gun was back there under a towel, but it'd been too late. Reg fired two shots into dude's head through the open window. Blaow! Blaow! He was so close, some of dude's blood splattered on the gun and Reg's hand. Reg then emptied his clip into dude's body, ending his existence. Blaow! Blaow! Blaow! Blaow! From the passenger side, Gee did basically the same, standing out the line of Reg's fire. With rapid succession, Gee emptied his clip into the body and head of the passenger. Blaow! Blaow! Blaow! Blaow! Blaow! Blaow! Reg and Gee then took a slow jog down the block to get off the street as quickly as possible. Gee tried to tuck the gun in his waistband but it was so hot it burned his skin. So he

70

tucked it under his t-shirt and kept it moving, as they both disappeared into the night.

This was the first time Reg and Gee actually took someone out. For Reg, it was a sense of relief, satisfaction, and revenge. For Gee, it was an act of undying loyalty to his best friend. He felt Reg's pain and rode with him, even if it meant doing twenty-five to life, or worse. He was right there by Reg's side, holding him down. It doesn't get much closer than that. Gee was his man. His right hand. His Nigga for Life.

A Star Is Born

Things went back to normal after the heat from the shooting died down. Everyone resumed their routine and life was smooth again. Later that summer, on a typical evening, TC and Lee had a dice game going in the park. HUNC, a guy from 140[th,] joined the game after a few. Sometimes when there was a game going on, niggas riding by would pull over and join in. That was a common occurrence back in the day. Any nigga that was getting money always drove through at least two blocks in Harlem; 114th between 8th and 7th for the chicks and 139th between Lenox and 7th for the action.

In the mid-to-late 80's, The Entertainers Basketball Tournament now held on 155[th]Street (known as The Rucker), used to be held in our park. Every major player in the game would come through to watch. Chicks would throw on their finest outfits and heels to stand in the park on concrete for hours waiting to be seen by someone, or everyone, for that matter. Everybody came through! Rich, Flaco, Kody, Eric Von Zip, just to name a few, but there were so many others. The list could go on and on. Then you had all the chicks niggas wanted to see. In every hood there was always what I called, "It Girls." These were the chicks whose names stayed on the tips of every nigga's tongue that was getting a few dollars back then. I'll let them remain anonymous but they know who they are.

But back to the summer of '92: niggas still drove through the block even though the tournament had gone for years; maybe out of habit. At this particular dice game, TC, Lee, and HUNC were going back and forth. There were others, but their paper wasn't long enough and they eventually dropped out leaving TC, Lee, and HUNC competing head to head. A major nigga from BK (Brooklyn), who'd migrated to Harlem named Jesus was driving by, saw the game and joined in. This nigga had some bread. I don't remember the play-by-play of this particular game but Lee sent his little brother, Lamont, to get five racks from the crib. Jesus went to his car a few times for five or ten.

Next thing you know, Iran "The Blade" Barkley, the reigning WBA Light Heavyweight Champion of the World, pulls up. He was just coming off a twelve-round victory over Thomas "Hitman" Hearns (Gee's favorite fighter) on March 20[th,] earlier that year; a triumph that had earned him a cool $500,000. He stops, joins the game and stops the bank. After a while, they change shit up. Jesus and HUNC have the bank together. Lee sends for another $10,000; these niggas are going at it! Iran goes to the glove compartment of what I believe was a brand new Lexus and got ten racks. This was the first time I ever saw money wrapped in bands from the bank. A nigga like me only saw street money in rubber bands up until then. His shit was all crisp $100 bills. A few minutes later, he was in that glove compartment again. That shit was bananas! The four of them went back and forth for hours. When all was said and done, Jesus and HUNC came out on top. I don't know the exact figure, but they had to have won upwards of fifty to sixty thousand dollars. Lee, TC and Iran took the "L" that day. But it was nothing; they would make that back in a day or so. That was one dice game I will never forget.

While the block is doing its normal day-to-day, Lee's little brother, Lamont, is coming into his own. Ever since he was young, he'd had a fascination with hip-hop. He was absolutely in love with it. Lamont would break-dance at the block parties and imitated rappers by lip-syncing their lyrics. It looked so cool because of how small he was.

Fast forward to his teenage years and his love of hip-hop blossomed into a full-blown passion; Lamont ate, slept, and breathed it. In his book, "Think Like A Success, Act Like A Success," Steve

Harvey says your gift exists because you do. Writing lyrics was Lamont's gift. Not his talent, his gift, and he was great at it. As a youngster, he always had hustle in him. After all, he had his older brothers and even his mom to thank for that. Although his mother kept him fresh and his brothers were deep in the drug game, Lamont worked for his own bread. He would wake up extra early and sell newspapers to earn his living, something that aided in building his character. Hard work was nothing new to him and through it all, Lamont never lost sight of his gift.

Always a fan of hip-hop, he studied the great ones until mastering his craft. Once, we all went to a show at NY's first hip-hop club, HomeBase, to see "Naughty By Nature" perform, where they debuted their song, "Hip-Hop Hooray." They killed it! After the show, Lamont said, "I can't fuck with him." But I think that was him looking at where he was sitting and where Treach was at the time. That didn't discourage Lamont one bit; he was determined to make his mark in the game. All he needed was a shot. Lamont knew he was nice and was determined to prove it. Eventually, he would get his chance.

Back in 1991, a talented lyricist from The Bx (the Bronx) by the name of Lord Finnesse, was having an autograph signing on 125th St. When Lamont heard about it, he made his way to the record store where it was being held. As Lord Finnesse finished, Lamont stepped to him and said, 'Yo, my name is Big L. I'm nice on the mic. Why don't you put me on?"(Lamont chose the name "Big L" because all his life he was known as "Lil' Lamont" or "Mont Mont." He wasn't little anymore and wanted to shed that "little" moniker forever. So from then on, everyone would address him as "Big L.") Finnesse looked at this skinny little kid and said, "Ok, I'll hook you up with my manager," in a dismissive tone. Big L said, "Listen, I'll rhyme for you right here and now and if you don't like it, I won't bother you again, ever!" Shiit, that was music to Finnesse's ears. He was looking for a reason not to like L. So Big L spit some bars and by the time he was done, Lord Finnesse was asking for L's number. And so it began.

Big L was on his way. From there, Lord Finnese introduced L to his crew, DITC (Digging in the Crates), which consisted of himself and his DJ, Mike Smooth, Showbiz and AG, OC, Diamond D, Buckwild, and rounding out the roster was none other than Fat Joe. They all were so impressed with Big L's lyrical skills, he was asked to join the crew. This was big for him; it felt good to be a part of such good company.

Big L couldn't wait for his time to shine. In the meantime, he practiced vigorously, perfecting his skills. Big L entered an amateur lyricist competition in 1992 and defeated almost 2,000 rappers with ease. After accepting all challenges from anybody, anywhere, at any time, his dues were paid. On top of that, being accepted into the DITC crew with open arms gave him the extra boost of confidence he needed. There was no stopping him. It was on!

After some studio sessions, Lord Finnesse felt L was ready and gave him a guest appearance on his 'Yes You May' remix. Big L got in the booth and murdered that shit! His first line was, "everywhere that I go everybody know my f'n name. I'm flooring niggas and I only weigh a buck and change." That was it; that was the beginning of what would become one of the baddest mf's to ever touch the mic.

In my eyes, a star was born. He made more guest appearances on a few tracks and built his notoriety as a budding underground artist. Now it was time to work on his first project.

A few months after the Wendy's incident, detectives picked Reg and Gee up, held them for questioning and put them in a lineup. According to detectives, an eyewitness identified them for the double homicide and they had to face a judge. At arraignment, they were charged and of course, plead not guilty. Now Reg and Gee had to sit in lockup until a trial or await some sort of plea deal the DA might offer. Of course, they separated the two in order to see if one would flip on the other, but that didn't work. So, off to The Island they went.

In '93, Rikers Island was a vicious environment for any mf to be in, even for those two. Back then, there was an influx of Latin King and Netas inmates on Rikers. Hispanics outnumbered other ethnic groups tremendously and more importantly, they held a united front against all enemies. If you weren't of Hispanic descent, your ass was under pressure on that island. Blacks couldn't use the phones; they were getting robbed, beat up, stabbed, slashed and all around abused in those jails. Something had to be done. The only way to fight back was to join forces and take a stand against the brutality that was being inflicted upon them. An inmate locked up in C73 who had West Coast affiliation with the "Miller Gangster Bloods" in Los Angeles named Omar "OG Mack" Portee, along with Leonard "OG Deadeye" MacKenzie, aligned to form the East Coast version of the United Blood Nation (UBN) on Rikers. The void of unity was filled and they took the Latin Kings and the Netas head-on in the NYC prison system. As UBN members were released, more members were recruited to form the original five sets of the East Coast facet of the Bloods. They consisted of the original UBN 183 Gangster Bloods, of the Bx, the 93 Gangster Bloods of Manhattan, the Gangster Killer Bloods, (G-Shine) of BK, the Valentine Bloods of Bx River Projects, and Sex Money Murder, also of the Bx's Soundview Projects, led by the infamous Peter (Pistol Pete) Rollack.

Gee was brought home (inducted) on the island, so he was part of the 93 Gangster Bloods. He had a few tiffs here and there but was able to hold his own. Once, while banging out with his homies, Gee received a scar from a razor on his nose that permanently damaged his otherwise handsome face. Reg, on the other hand maintained a neutral status while on the Rock. He never subscribed to any gang affiliation. Having done time previously, he was well known throughout the NYC and NYS prison systems. Reg linked up with veterans of the system who were well-respected and didn't conform to gang recruitment.

One of those seasoned veterans was a fearsome OG out of BK, named Walter "Tut" Johnson. He's the same Tut that 2Pac spoke about in his song, 'Against All Odds,' off the Makavelli LP where he said, "Gunshots to Tut, now you stuck." Rapper 50 Cent also made mention of him in 'Many Men' off the 2003 'Get Rich or Die Trying' LP. It included the line, "Feds ain't know jack when Pac got shot, I got a kite from the pen saying Tut got knocked." 2Pac himself accused Tut of the Quad Studio shooting in which he was shot five times and robbed of around $40,000 worth of jewelry. Later, he was also accused of the iconic rapper's murder, of which he claims his innocence in both charges. Having spent a considerable amount of his early adult life in and out of prison, he was very well known. Tut's name rang bells wherever he stepped foot. Niggas got in formation for that mf. So Reg and Tut became cool with one another on The Island. Alliances like that proved to be beneficial then and in the long run.

After months of sitting on Rikers, although unattainable, they were given a bail. Now the lawyers had to work at getting the bail reduced, so Reg and Gee had to sit some more. Finally, the judge granted a bail the families could come up with. Reg got out first and after a couple of months, Gee made bail as well.

The two of them were back out on the street. Now it was time to do some homework. Who the fuck was this so called eyewitness? They wouldn't have to wait long for the answer. At one of Reg and Gee's prior court dates, TC stood in the hallway of 100 Centre Street waiting to return to court after lunch. Gee's man, who shall remain anonymous, was walking by trying not to be noticed. TC saw him and said, "What's up? You know Gee and Reg have court today."

The guy replied nervously, "Oh, word?"

Then he kept walking toward the elevators like he was in a hurry. TC found that to be kind of strange. Gee was supposed to be his man and he was facing a double homicide. I don't know about you, but I think his man should've showed just a little more concern than, "Oh word." I know I would've, but that's just me. Obviously TC felt the same. Later, when he saw Gee's man he asked him why he was downtown at the courthouse.

The guy said, "Nah. I was coming from probation."

This really raised TC's eyebrows because at the time, the probation department wasn't on that floor. TC knew this mf was lying, and he was determined to get to the bottom of this shit. At Reg and Gee's next court date, TC made it his business to walk down the corridor in the direction Gee's man came from the last time. He couldn't tell what was behind the door because it wasn't labeled, but acting like he was lost, he asked a gentleman who exited the room if that was the probation department.

He replied, "No, probation isn't on this floor."

TC said, "Damn, so what's this?"

The man confided, "I'm not supposed say, but it's one of the DA's offices."

TC politely thanked the gentleman and walked back to the courtroom to wait for Reg and Gee's case to be called. He couldn't wait for them to hit the street. Now that they were out on bail, TC was able to feed them the info about Gee's man. It turned out he caught a charge and gave the police a statement about the Wendy's shooting to save his own ass. Gee was f'd up when he heard that his man was a rat, but Reg wasn't. After receiving the info, he gave TC that look and TC knew what time it was. Not long after that, Gee's man was no more. Just like that.

Reg and Gee's troubles weren't over yet. They still had the case looming over their heads. The absence of an eyewitness made the case weaker but didn't make it disappear. The battle still had to be won in court. Now, at least they got to fight the case on the outside of the gate, or so they thought.

After being on the street for about a year, Reg and Gee were stopped and detained going through the metal detectors in the lobby of 100 Centre Street before making it up to the courtroom. Immediately, they thought about the missing witness. Unbeknownst to them, it was for a murder and attempted murder charge in Brooklyn. Niggas were baffled because Reg and Gee never did any dirt out in BK. This shit was getting weirder by the minute. After being cuffed in the lobby, they were taken up to the courtroom and the judge was informed of the new charges against them. The judge revoked their bail and remanded them.

Back to Rikers they went. After a month or so, Reg was released; the BK charges were dropped for lack of evidence. Gee,

79

however was held after being chosen in a lineup. None of this shit was true, but what could he do? Gee had to sit up while he proved his innocence. This new arrest was just a ploy used by the DA and detectives to get Gee to turn on Reg. They felt Reg was guilty of the Wendy's shooting because he had motive and they were furious about losing their eyewitness, so this was payback. They told Gee they would pin the BK and Wendy's charges on him if he didn't give Reg up. "Look out for yourself," is what they urged. "He already told us you did it. Why do you think he's home and you're not? That should tell you something."

Gee was unwavering. That TV cop shit wasn't going to work on him. He was prepared to sit up and fight as long as it took. Gee sat on Rikers for almost two years fighting his cases, going back and forth to court for both. Taking the BK case to trial was an uphill battle but there was no way he was copping to that shit. He lawyered up and prepared to wage war with the NYS Criminal Justice System. I don't remember how long the trial lasted, but in the end he was the victor.

Gee beat the charges on a technicality. The attempted murder victim testified that the shooter had stood behind him so closely, his breath was felt on the back of his neck. Gee's attorney asked the victim how tall he was. The victim replied, "6'3."

"Are you sure you felt the shooter's breath on the back of your neck before getting shot?" the attorney probed.

"Yes," the victim replied.

"Are you positive?" the attorney asked again.

"Yes, he came up behind me and told me not to move. He was so close I felt his breath on my neck. Then, he shot me. I'm positive," insisted the victim.

The attorney replied, "I find that difficult to believe because my client is only five-foot nine." He presented Gee's pedigree card as evidence. Then he announced, "In order for my client to breathe on the back of your neck, he would've had to be wearing four-inch heels. Unless you're telling me my client was in drag when he shot you and killed your friend, I think you might want to reconsider your statement."

The audience let out a little chuckle.

"Are you calling my client a cross dresser?" the attorney asked incredulously.

Before the victim could answer, the audience burst into laughter. The victim eventually denied it. It may have seemed like Gee was in the clear, but the DA pushed and pushed, presenting more and more evidence, witnesses, and so-called facts to the attention of the court. The trial went on for another few days but that was what really convinced the jury that Gee was not the shooter.

The jury ultimately declared him "not guilty" and Gee was released immediately from the courtroom, and his bail was reinstated for the Wendy's shooting. It was a small triumph, but Reg and Gee still had a hill to climb. It seemed like the Wendy's charge was never going to go away but eventually that case would get dropped as well. Lack of evidence and no witnesses forced the DA to finally let it go. It was about f'n time!

Niggas could finally get on with their lives. As Big L was in the lab working on his album, NFL was building a momentum of their own. Having had success with the Memorial Day game, we decided to jump into the party arena too. The goal was to throw another basketball game, following up with an after-party. After the fiasco in the spring, The One 4 One Crew wasn't interested in playing us again; no way, now how.

Reg and TC reached out to Same Gang. They were one of the crews who made their mark on the Harlem Party circuit. D Ferg (short for Darold Ferguson) was the go-to man for that type of shit. He was at the forefront of their crew. I wouldn't necessarily call him the boss; he was just the most well-known member, in my opinion. D Ferg is also the father of a very popular and successful rapper, known to you as ASAP Ferg. He's doing very well for himself and I'm sure his dad would be proud. Sadly, we lost D Ferg to kidney failure in 2003, but before his passing, he owned a boutique in Harlem and was mainly known for printing logos and shirts for various record labels, including Bad Boy, Teddy Riley, Heavy D & The Boyz, Bell Biv Devoe, and many others. Ferg, as he was commonly known, was also responsible for 90% of any printed t-shirts that went on in Harlem at one point. So, when Reg, Lee and TC approached him about a game with NFL and an opportunity to print the shirts, he gladly accepted. Bam! NFL was in the party game!

With Same Gang on the flyer, it was sure to be a hit since they already had a following. This time, the game was held at the world famous Gauchos Gym located on Gerard Ave and 149th Street in the Bx. This gym is where almost all NYC basketball players (there are too many to mention) honed their skills under the tutelage of founder, Lou d'Almeida. D Ferg was in pocket for the game jerseys but we needed something to set us apart from the rest of the crews.

Once again, TC came up with the idea for all members to wear NFL jerseys, but not the bullshit ones found at Modell's those were replicas. We used to go downtown to Cosby's, an official sports memorabilia store located in Madison Square Garden to get the official ones worn by the players. It was ingenious! We were the only crew with an identifiable uniform.

Another thing we did differently was use a theme song. Before our team was announced, the DJ was instructed to play 'Niggaz for Life,' by NWA. When the song dropped, the team ran onto the court and started the layup line. Every player had a different NFL jersey on over their basketball jersey. That shit looked crazy! No one was expecting to see anything like that and we killed it! The turnout was great due to Same Gang's popularity. I can't front, no one really knew about us, so the people really came to see them. Now all we had to do was win the game; but not so fast... them niggas busted our asses! It wasn't a blowout, but a loss nevertheless.

The game was over, now on to the after party. We rented buses to take everyone out to "The Rink," an extremely popular roller skating rink located in Bergenfield, NJ. Now it was time to get our skate on! It was a beautiful night; everyone had fun. Now when people thought about dudes from 139th St, they could associate us with parties instead of all the street shit niggas were involved in. That's what we were aiming for; trying to shed that negative image. People felt more at ease being in our midst, instead of feeling like they had to watch us with the side eye. It was a good feeling.

Eventually, more basketball games and parties would ensue, in an attempt to build our own following. We had a game against Same Gang at Gauchos around Easter. TC's brain was always working overtime and he decided we were going to throw small stuffed bunnies to the ladies in the crowd as we ran onto the gym floor with our theme song playing. The ladies loved it! D Ferg, using his music industry connections had a surprise for them as well. At halftime, Horace Brown, a popular R&B singer at Uptown Records performed his hit single, 'Taste Your Love.' My girl at the time was in the audience with all of her friends and they went wild! Now, all we had to do was finish out the second half and take the victory. But no; another f'n "L" was added to our record. But it was all good. The evening was pulled off without a hitch and that's what counted.

NFL felt it was time to start making some money from the parties. We needed to find a venue large enough to hold a decent crowd but not big so as to make it look empty if enough people didn't attend. We settled on a Sports Bar in the Bx located on Tremont Ave. It was the perfect size for our first party with the NFL name appearing on the flier, solo. This party was also a success. The next day, everybody was talking about some chick that resembled Halle Berry. Rel Mack from "The Best Out" even came to the block asking where we found her. I personally didn't see her but she was all niggas were talking about. The crazy shit is, no one ever saw her again. It was like she was a ghost. Anyway, we had our first successful party without the following of any other crew. It was based solely on our own merit. Everyone had a good time and was looking forward to our next event. NFL was finally included in the Harlem party circuit.

Lee, Reg, and TC were doing their one-two step in the street. The arrangement Reg and TC had still stood as long as he was able to get his hands on work. Things were going well. But of course we know, good things don't last for long. Niggas from 139th and 140th were always cool with one another. It was almost like we combined the two blocks and made one enormous family. The only thing separating us was the park.

A guy from that block named Mike was hustling out of one of the buildings over there. He sold dust, more commonly known as

PCP, a highly hallucinogenic drug which comes in various forms such as, pills, powder, or a liquid. In some areas it's called 'Dips', or 'Dippers', 'Wet', 'Leaky Leak', or many other names. In 140th Street the liquid form was sold. Mike would pour a certain amount of the liquid into a jar, add mint leaves and shake the jar until they were perfectly blended, scooping small amounts of the mixture into tiny weed bags. Mike was killing them; he made a lot of money off that shit. His hustle was different from most because he had no real competition. The closest crew selling dust was blocks away, as opposed to niggas selling crack, who had competitors all around them. His shit was smooth sailing for the most part.

Mike shared the building with another guy who sold crack. (Let's just call him Sunday.) No problems there. Mike had his clientele and Sunday had his. The problem only arose when the people Sunday was getting work from wanted to take the building. These people had a reputation for violence if presented with resistance. But Sunday was no pushover. He was an older guy who made his bones in the street and was respected for it. The people I mentioned didn't care about anyone's reputation. They could care less if people respected or loved you. It was their way or no way. These people were ruthless; and they didn't give a fuck! These people had a name, and they called themselves, "The Lynch Mob."

If you lived in Harlem in the early-to-mid 90's, you knew exactly who they were. Before they became The Lynch Mob they were just a crew that got money on 142nd St. As mentioned earlier, the brains behind the crew was Fatboy. He was a super cool dude. All he did was get money, buy cars and clothes, and a lot of gambling. By the mid 90's, Fatboy and his crew was known as one of the most dangerous crews in Harlem. Committing murder after murder, their body count grew almost as fast as the commas in their safes. TLM struck terror in the hearts of most west Harlem niggas. Under his domination, Fatboy directed TLM to conquer as much territory as they possibly could. And conquer they did. Their headquarters were on 142nd and Lenox Ave on the downtown side. From there, they controlled niggas in 143rd Street, and of course 142nd, 141st, 140th, 138th, 137th, 136th, 134th, and 133rd, that I know of. There were probably more I don't know about. His tactic was to give a nigga in a block some work. Most of the time that worked well because Fatboy was known for having bread and niggas would be eager to hop aboard a ship that was already sailing. But if niggas f'd up the work and couldn't pay, Fatboy would take the spot. Sometimes, if he really wanted the spot, he would give a nigga some f'd up work, knowing it would put them in debt. When they couldn't pay, he took the spot. If they offered resistance, The Lynch Mob offered them lead.

If you go back and look at the territory on the list, you'll notice two blocks are missing. One is 135th St. To my knowledge, no one hustled in that block anyway. The other block was 139th St. For some reason, the two crews had a mutual respect for one another. Don't get me wrong, if Fatboy wanted our block, his Lynch Mob was strong enough to show up. But it would've been an all-around bad situation. Yes, Fatboy was strong, but he couldn't do it alone.

That strength came from a powerful man named, Jason (Jase) Biggs. Around that time, Jason Biggs was one of the most feared niggas on the streets of Harlem. He moved smoothly around Harlem in his white Mazda MPV like a hot knife through butter. Jase was another super cool dude, unless you had a problem with him; he stood at the helm of many other shooters. One he was particularly close with was a guy named Terrence Chisum. He was another gunslinger whose reputation for violence preceded him. With the mind of a CEO and the manpower of a small military platoon, there wasn't much that could stop these niggas.

Some of you may say there were other crews TLM wasn't f'n with. I'll say this: there were definitely others like Preacher's Crew, The Vigilantes, Doo Wop's Crew, and Jim Ice's Crew. Niggas wasn't f'n with them either but if a beef occurred, there would've been casualties on both sides. I'm pretty sure The Lynch Mob would've held their own.

Let's get back to the Mike situation and the building. I just wanted to paint a vivid picture of what he was up against, f'g with those Lynch Mob mfs. Mike wasn't the violent type. All he wanted was money, cars, clothes, jewelry, and to have a good time. If any bullshit came his way, he would crease. He knew there was nothing he could do to stop Fatboy and Jase, so he went to Lee for assistance. Lee didn't care for Fatboy or Jase. He told Reg and TC about the situation because he knew he needed backup for these mfs.

One day, while chilling in the park, Lee noticed Jase's MPV slowly ride down 140thand stop in front of Mike's building. He knew what time it was. Lee went to get his ratchet (gun), and urged Reg and TC to do the same and meet back in the park. The three of them made their way through the park to 140th. Jase was standing on the stoop talking to Mike as Lee approached and asked Mike if he was okay. Before he could respond Jase said, "He's good. Why, what's up?"

Lee said, "I wasn't talking to you."

"Well I'm talking to you. Like I said, he's good!" Jase replied firmly. Seeing the situation about to escalate, Reg immediately stepped in. All three of them were strapped and Jase kept his thing on him. That shit could've gotten ugly real quick! Reg told Jase, Mike
87

already let them know about what was going on and they couldn't just take the building like that. Jase said, "Yo, Reg, niggas put in work for this building. You know how this shit goes."

Reg said, "Okay, but you still gotta let the man live. He gotta eat the same as you do."

Jase thought about it, agreeing, "Ok, you got a point. Ima let it slide for now." Then he hopped in the MPV and drove off. Mike's predicament was diffused for the moment and he hoped it would stay that way; lucky for him it did.

You see, Jase and Reg had a rapport. A rapport Lee didn't appreciate and he really didn't like the fact that Jase seemed to have more respect for Reg than him. That level of narcissism was both frightening and extremely dangerous. It burned his ego like a three alarm fire, to the point he began to resent Reg. That resentment would eventually grow into a deep rooted hatred. Lee was a jealous mf. He didn't like Fatboy because of the power and money he possessed and he didn't like Jase because of the reputation he had in Harlem. Jase's name rang bells in the hood and Lee wanted that recognition. He wanted people to revere him the same way.

Lee was eager to get into a beef with Fatboy and Jase. It was like he wanted any small situation to escalate so he could try and prove Jase wasn't all that tough. Niggas couldn't see it at first, but Jase did. He caught up with Reg later and explained the real reason he was putting pressure on Mike. Jase told Reg how Mike hid the fact that he had been paying him for protection the whole time they were locked up. Now that they were home, Mike started acting funny and felt he didn't have to pay anymore. This infuriated Jase and made him apply even more pressure.

After the issue with Sunday was taken care of, Jase figured he would really crush Mike by staying in his pockets and taking his livelihood for trying to play him. Jase didn't give a fuck who was behind Mike, he only eased the pressure off of him on the strength of Reg and TC. Reg reasoned with him again and asked if he would back off permanently. Jase agreed, only on the strength of their bond. He said, "Ima leave that nigga alone, but y'all better get some money outta that faggot mf! And your man Lee, he's on some bullshit. Y'all better talk to that nigga."

All TC could do is shake his head. On another occasion, Fatboy came through 139th and picked TC up in the whip. After some small talk, he brought the Mike situation up and the conversation they had with Jase. He expressed his concern about Lee's approach. Fatboy saw Lee as a potential problem down the line. He knew he could reason with TC and Reg, but Lee was a different story. Fatboy always had love for TC and wanted to keep the peace. He offered TC $40,000 to basically look the other way while he sent his people to take care of Lee.

"Are you f'n crazy?! I ain't doin no shit like that!" TC exclaimed.

Fatboy looked at him, smiling, "You know what? That's why I love you, nigga. Another mf would've gave their mama up for that kind of bread, but not you. That's some real nigga shit."

TC went on to make it clear, "I'm not them niggas."

Fatboy reached into the center console and handed TC $5,000 wrapped neatly in three rubber bands.

"What's this for? I don't need your money. I'm good," TC assured him.

89

Fatboy looked at him and said sternly, "Listen, take this money. It don't mean shit. It's a gift from me to you but I wanna say something to you. I exposed how I feel about that mf, so I can't do shit to him now because I know how you feel about him, too. But mark my word, that nigga is gonna be the death of y'all."

Fatboy pulled over, shook TC's hand and let him out of the ride. They were all the way downtown, so TC had to take a cab back to the block. On the way back uptown, his head was spinning. At first he felt insulted for Fatboy even thinking he would betray Lee like that. Then he thought back to how Lee stole from him and Reg previously and how selfish Lee could be at times. Maybe Fatboy was right about Lee. As f'd up as he felt, TC kept the conversation with Fatboy under wraps. The love he had for Lee overruled any amount of money.

No matter how f'd up a person may be, love can blind you. It's like a woman that's being abused by her man; everyone around her can see it, but she won't until she hits rock bottom and hopefully it's not too late when she does. This was exactly the way it was with Lee. Niggas loved him. It was just that simple.

Big L was on his grind trying to put his first album together. Lord Finnesse had him under his wing long enough. He believed in L's talent and took him everywhere he went to get as much exposure as possible. When Finnesse had an interview, Big L had an interview. When Lord Finnesse had a show, Big L had a show. He'd let L get twenty minutes to spit on a set and he'd kill it.

Mfs knew he was destined to be a star from the first time he hit the stage. Kicking the craziest rhymes, the illest compounds, the most clever punch lines, and on top of all that, he had a commanding stage presence that solidified his place in the hearts of Finnesse and the rest of the DITC Crew, which was no easy feat. If you weren't from their hood in the Bx, you couldn't be down, PERIOD. But that went out the window when Big L came into the picture. He proved himself to his DITC comrades and now it was time to show the world.

In 1992, Big L was scheduled for an interview at WKCR 89.9, on "The Stretch and Bobbito Show," a late-night underground radio show that helped artists such as Nas, Jay-Z, Wu Tang and many others get their start. This was the first time the world heard Big L's voice live and on the radio. Shows like "Stretch and Bobbito" was where artists would get that figurative stamp of approval from true hip-hop fans everywhere.

The world was listening and Big L had a lot to say. After making a solid impression, L was always welcomed back to the radio show. One of his most memorable visits was when he showed up with Jay-Z. Both still early in their careers, the two went line for line in front of the entire listening audience, proving themselves to be lyrical beasts and putting on a poetic display of genius. It was an informal battle but they would never have admitted it if asked. But they did have an actual battle, right on Lenox between 140th and 141st streets. This was one for the record books. Too bad we didn't have the cell phone technology of today to capture that epic bout. That shit would be priceless right now! After it was all said and done, those in attendance said it was a tie. I was there and I tend to agree. Big L definitely held his own against a young Jay-Z, who is now arguably one of the greatest rappers, ever. So if Jay got better, L undoubtedly would've done the same.

News spread all through the hood about the Big L/Jay-Z battle. Radio interviews and public appearances only boosted his already-growing buzz. A few of his friends caught mic fever and set out to join Big L on his quest for hip-hop stardom and L obliged them. He was a major influence on all the local rappers who were trying to get on. When they saw the success Big L was having, it really pushed them over the edge. If niggas didn't know what they wanted to be when they grew up before, they knew now for sure! Dudes like Killa Cam (now Cam'ron), Murda Mase (now Ma$e), Herb McGruff, and Took Da Boss were undoubtedly influenced to take the musical route seriously. Shit, Cam and Ma$e were ballplayers, and good ones at that. But it wasn't enough to hold their attention after being bitten by the rap bug. They formed a group consisting of Murda Mase, Killa Cam, Digga and Bloodshed (RIP), called "Caged Fury." They approached Big L a few times asking him to be down with them but he was busy with his own affairs. Then they asked McGruff. When he joined, L basically relented and joined as well. Following his lead, the group probably changed their name to "Children of The Corn" because of Big L's love of horror flicks. He still repped DITC, but had enough credibility to start his own movement.

L had half a dozen MC's ready to emulate him and he didn't even have a deal yet. That was something! But a deal wasn't far off. Although Lord Finnesse discovered Big L and was most instrumental in guiding his career up to that point, it was rapper Tim Dog who actually walked him into the office of Kurt Woodley, then A&R at Columbia Records. Tim Dog was an underground rapper whose claim to fame was the controversial dis song, 'Fuck Compton!' aimed at Dr. Dre, NWA, and a host of other West Coast artists. He knew how dope Big L was and wanted Kurt to meet him. Kurt impressed with Big L's lyrical skills to say the least. He introduced L to Faith Newman, another A&R at Columbia who had just signed Nas, Kurious, and Jamalski. She was placed in charge of Columbia's hip-hop division where she created a movement called, 'No Doubt'.

This endeavor would include the aforementioned artists, plus The Fugees. After hearing him flow, Big L would come to close out the lineup.

They loved him at Columbia. The label was a giant in the record industry but they weren't too big on hip-hop back then. Columbia hadn't grown to fully understand and appreciate the music and its potential. Back then, they would give an artist like Big L a small demo budget of like $5,000 to cut a few tracks. If they liked any of them, Columbia would select a single and send it to radio to see if it could create a buzz. This is the deal they gave Lord Finnesse for Big L.

Now it was time to go to work. Being a member of DITC had its perks. L automatically had production from Finnesse and Showbiz, but he also got work from Patrick Moxey, the owner of Ultra, one if the biggest EDM labels around. Back then, Patrick was working with Gang Starr at Payday Records and that connection afforded Big L the opportunity to have production from DJ Premier on his first project. Not bad for a neophyte.

Big L's work ethic was crazy. He had notebooks of rhymes in his stash just ready to go. His brain always worked overtime. If you paid attention, you would catch L mouthing words to himself after he spoke. He would actually do this in the middle of a conversation, always trying to find ways to flip the way he normally spoke into witty, clever rhymes in his head.

When it was time to step in the booth, Big L was more than ready. Most of his shit was done in one take. L practiced so much in his free time, he had shit memorized, so there was no need to waste time writing in the studio. There was no need for three and four takes when he stepped in the booth; it was all in his head. The man was focused and determined to be the best. Big L recorded track after track; and after narrowing them down to a few, he put the songs together to complete his demo. L didn't have to shop his demo like most artists; all he had to do was take it to Columbia, who was anxiously anticipating its arrival. One of the tracks was a morbidly horrifying song called, 'The Devil's Son,' in which Big L explains to Showbiz, the producer, how he dreamt he was the offspring of Satan. It starts off with the Nas sample from Main Source's 'Live at the BBQ,' that said, "When I was twelve I went to hell for snuffing Jesus." It then followed with Nas's sample from MC Serch's 'Back To The Grill' that stated, "I'm waving automatic guns at nuns." After Big L finished the song, Showbiz looked at him and asked, "Are you really gonna say that shit?"

L just smiled and said, "Yeah."

That was that. They put a few more songs together and the demo was complete. When they took it to Columbia, Showbiz was kind of nervous. He knew the execs had never heard anything like that before. Shit, *he* never heard anything like that before! They played 'The Devil's Son' for the execs at the label and they f'n loved it! They absolutely loved it.

Big L was on his way. Columbia released the single in 1993. Now it was time to finish the project. He would go on to lay twelve tracks on his debut album entitled, 'Lifestylez ov da Poor & Dangerous', released in 1995. Of the twelve tracks, three singles were put out. The first was a collaboration with the legendary DJ Kid Capri called, 'Put It On'. Big L once again showed us his lyrical gift with punch lines like, "And when it comes to getting nookie, I'm not a rookie. I got girls make that chick Toni Braxton look like Whoopi."

Followed by a video, 'Put It On' had Big L's name hot in the streets. I remember the first time I heard it on the radio. I couldn't believe it! It may seem like I'm making a big deal about it, but back then it was. Even though Big L wasn't involved in that life, he came from where we came from. He was one of us. To hear his voice on the air had me f'd up! I was so proud and happy for my nigga! We all were; the whole NFL. Big L's hard work had finally paid off. It seemed like success was right around the corner but he'd soon find there was no time to bask in the glory.

Big L was already looking forward to his next single being released and there was no time to sit still. Next up was 'MVP.' The initials stood for Most Valuable Poet, and a valuable poet he was. It contained a sample from the very popular single, 'Stay with Me,' by DeBarge, a successful Motown act in the 80'sthat included Took Da Boss on the hook. Right after 'MVP' was released, The Notorious BIG, the rap phenomenon from BK who was signed to Bad Boy Records, released a remix to his single, 'One More Chance,' off his debut album, "Ready To Die," using the same DeBarge sample. Only his had more of a mellow feel to it. (It's my favorite rap song of all time.) I mentioned to Big L that his producers should've smoothed the sample out and people would've probably been more receptive to it. L was instantly annoyed by my suggestion. He defended his producers, as well he should have. Big L was loyal to DITC and that's the way it was supposed to be and I respected him one hundred percent for that. Biggie had major success with this single, selling over one million copies by July of 1995.

Big L was not one to take a backseat to any other rapper. He went back to the lab and replaced the old sample with a totally new track, kept the lyrics, and dropped the 'MVP Remix' with an accompanying video. His super-slick talk over the smoothed out track made it a listening pleasure. With lyrics like "I'll run up like Machine Gun Kelly with a black skully, put one in your belly, leave you smelly, then take your Pelle Pelle", floating over that melodic track almost made you forget this nigga just shot you in the stomach and robbed you for your leather jacket; it was just that smooth. Then there was 'No Endz, No Skinz'; it was the 90's version of Kanye West's 'Gold Digger', off his 2005 "Late Registration" album. Big L spit rhymes about women who won't even consider a man's advances if he doesn't have money. In other words, "no romance without finance." One of his most memorable lines is, "They wanna know why I'm so fly, a girl asked me for a ring and I put one around her whole eye." L was the compound king! Out of the three singles, 'No Endz, No Skinz' got the least amount of airplay.

But other tracks had tremendous underground success. Songs like, '8 Iz Enuff' which featured a young Herb McGruff and Killa Cam. Also, 'Da Graveyard' featuring a young Jay-Z and a host of other MC's who ganged up on the track to make it an underground classic. Last, but not least, was 'Danger Zone', an ode to 139th and Lenox. This track really represented Big L's horrorcore style. There was no video, no radio play, no promotion, and it's probably the song he's remembered for the most. 'Danger Zone' captured Big L's fascination with evil and mayhem. I'm not sure if he was an atheist but he acted like he'd been tight with Satan since the 3rd grade. I'm pretty sure it was done for shock-value.

Like the brilliant lyricist Eminem, Big L had a penchant for making jaws drop. Some of the shit this mf said could make a convict blush. For example, "I'm choking enemies til they start turning pale. Satan said I'm learning well, Big L's gonna burn in Hell." Another: "I'm on some satanic shit strictly. Lil kids be waking up cryin, yellin, Mommy, Big L is coming to get me!" Other lines were worse. The song was incredible and the concept was dope; lyrics like those made you think he was the Stephen King of hip-hop. But that was Big L. You had to love him.

'Lifestylez of da Poor & Dangerous' will always be an underground classic, although that wasn't the goal. Big L wanted popular success without having to sacrifice his style in the process. The fact that Eminem reached superstar status with the same style, proved Big L was ahead of his time. In fact, he may have predicted this fact with this line, "I'm so far ahead of my time, my parents haven't met yet", from '7 Minute Freestyle' with Jay-Z. So why couldn't Big L achieve equal or greater prosperity than Eminem?

Underground hip-hop loved him. Even Columbia loved him. They just didn't know what to do with him because the mainstream wasn't ready. Big L's album debuted at 149 on the US Billboard 200 and number 22 on R&B/Hip-Hop albums. As of 2000, the album has sold 200,000 copies according to Nielsen Soundscan. For a first-timer, the album didn't necessarily flop. It did what was expected, considering the promo, or lack thereof, from Columbia. It's my thought that his art was overshadowed by the bigger acts signed to the label at that time. Columbia was focused on Nas's 'Illmatic' and The Fugees were a main priority there as well. Those were some big acts Big L had to follow. With Kurt Woodley leaving Columbia for an all-label deal with RCA, no one was there to push Big L's music. At the time, Faith Newman was all tied up with Nas's career, and that would've been a conflict of interest. Sort of like working for UPS but helping Fed Ex out at the same time.

The bottom line is, Columbia was too corporate for Big L's style. There was no one left at the label to communicate with him; No one to push his music. Columbia was too afraid. The executives would say, "Oh, it's too raw and gritty for radio, or Top 30." If L would've been given that one crossover song, he could've survived at Columbia but that didn't happen and the relationship at the label was strained.

While Big L was at odds with Columbia, NFL was moving forward with parties and basketball games. Now when the team ran onto the court, we had Big L's 'Danger Zone' as a bona-fide anthem to go with 'Niggaz For Life' from NWA. It also gave our crew star-quality to have a recognized rapper in our midst. Big L even gave NFL a shout out at the end of '8 Iz Enuff', solidifying our name on wax forever.

While things were not going so well for L, a great opportunity fell in the hands of another NFL member. The owner of Gus's Bar had passed away and the family shut the place down. This left everyone who hustled there with no place to make their money, causing a major setback. Black Tone turned this negative into a positive by making an offer to buy the bar. It was definitely a strategic move on his part. Having complete ownership of the bar, Black Tone could dictate who and what would be sold in his spot.

After negotiating extensively, Tone struck a deal for an undisclosed amount, making him the new sole proprietor of the bar. With outdated deco, he planned to remodel, wanting to give it a more contemporary flair; this was going to require some bread. Black Tone was already in a f'd up situation with no place to hustle and he'd just dropped a huge chunk of his stash for the bar purchase. He needed a plan.

Tone went a couple of doors down to the grocery store owned by Arabs and arranged to finagle a deal to hustle in the back of the store for six months until he got the bar renovated. The Arabs agreed, for a small fee of course, to which Black Tone eagerly obliged. He knew the amount of money the bar could potentially make and he wasn't letting anything stand in the way of progress.

Soon the flow was coming back as his clientele found him set up in the store, where he worked the hours from six to twelve. After twelve, everything was sold from behind bulletproof glass. If you're not from the hood, I need to clarify: at 12am, a 24-hour store would close their doors and operate behind thick glass like the kind found in a bank. A patron would place their money in a compartment located on a turntable and had to spin it around to the store clerk who in turn would fill the order and spin it back to the patron. (I say all of this because it has relevance later.)

Working for only six hours, Black Tone was still able to average $2,500-$3,000 a night. I remember one night he made $6,000 in those six hours. Shit, at that pace, the bar would be open in no time. If he did that in the store, imagine what the bar would do once it opened? He couldn't wait. Renovations began and Tone was focused. Every day he was on deck, making sure shit was going according to plan. Of course, news about the new ownership circulated quickly through the hood and people stopped by to chat and wished Tone luck with his new venture. The bar was a staple in our hood where people could go to unwind, have a drink and socialize in peace, for the most part.

It wasn't as popular as other big name Harlem spots, but it was still on the map. Cuba Gooding Sr., lead singer of The Main Ingredient, responsible for the hits, 'Just Don't Want To Be Lonely' and 'Everybody Plays The Fool' would frequent Gus's when he was in town, and the regulars loved him. The neighborhood was sad to see Gus's close, but were thrilled to know it was reopening thanks to Black Tone. Everyone was happy for him. Well, almost everyone.

One day, during the renovation process, Reg and TC were chilling in the bar with Black Tone; he was trying to get them to help clean up a little but they weren't having that. After a while, Lee walked in, stood in the doorway, put his hands on his hips as he looked around and said, "Yeah my nigga, shit lookin real good up in here. Lemme see, Pebbles (RIP) is gonna be on this side, Bo is gonna be on this side, you're on this side, what side am I on?"

Black Tone stopped sweeping, looked at Lee and said in a loud, boisterous voice, "YOU ON THE OUT-SIDE MF, 'CUZ YO ASS AIN'T COMIN UP IN HERE!" Reg and TC burst out in a gut wrenching laugh. Reg almost fell off the barstool and TC spit out his drink. Lee was furious and embarrassed, and Reg and TC laughing didn't help. Lee had a habit of biting his lip when he was pissed and he almost chewed his whole lip off at this. That nigga was tight! He stood there for a second, turned, and walked out.

TC knew it was on from there; he knew Lee was going to be a thorn in Black Tone's side from then on. Somehow, he was going to be a problem. Why, you may ask? Didn't Lee already have a steady flow of income coming from the park? The answer is yes. Didn't he say no one else could hustle in the park, whether you're from the block or not? The answer to that is yes, as well. So what the fuck did he need to put coke in the bar with Black Tone for? Shit, Tone couldn't sell crack in the park! Why? Because Lee said so! I won't say the man was greedy, but what would you call it? I'm not going to say Lee was jealous of the fact that Black Tone was able to purchase the bar, putting him in the position for maximum earning potential, I'll let you make the call.

Remember, Gus's was a cocaine gold mine. Lee knew this and he wanted in. When Black Tone denied him access, it infuriated him. Lee couldn't just bully his way in. Tone wasn't having that. So

100

basically, Lee wouldn't be going into the cocaine business, at least not in *that* bar. And that was that. Or was it?

Lee's mom would sometimes organize parties and social gatherings where everyone from the block was welcome. At one particular function, Black Tone was in attendance with the mother of his four daughters (may she RIP). The party was going smoothly until Black Tone noticed how she was dancing with Don, Lee's brother. Tone approached her, they had words and he sent her home. It was a small situation that was diffused before getting out of hand. No one got hurt, no one died, simple. No big deal, right? Well, it wasn't until Lee got involved.

The next day, he stepped to Black Tone and accused him of disrespecting his mother's party. Tone looked at Lee like he was crazy, replying dismissively, "My nigga, all I did was grab my baby mother and take her out the joint. How the fuck did I disrespect your mom's party?"

"Because you did, mf! I said you did!" Lee insisted.

Black Tone wasn't trying to argue with him so he went about his business. Lee wasn't trying to let it ride though. Later that day, he brought Don around to Lenox Ave where Black Tone was sitting in front of the bar. Lee wanted them to fight and Tone knew what time it was as soon as he saw them come around the corner. When Don got close enough, without saying a word, he threw a punch, hitting Tone in the side of his face. It was on; the two men started scrapping! Keep in mind, Black Tone was still f'd up from a shoulder injury he'd suffered a few months earlier so he wasn't one hundred percent. But that didn't stop him from holding his own. Somehow, he was able to get Don on the ground and starting f'n him up. Don did his best to cover his face as Tone swung repeatedly. As a crowd gathered, Reg saw it was getting out of hand. Always a peacemaker, he broke the fight up, pulling Black Tone off of Don. After the two men were separated, Reg gave Lee a look like, *what the fuck is wrong with you?!*

Lee must have read Reg's mind because he said, "You know what the fuck this nigga did. He disrespected my mom's joint last night!"

The reality of it was, Black Tone didn't even cause much of a disturbance when he escorted his baby's mother out of the party. So where was the disrespect? Was it about the party at all? Or was it backlash for being denied entry into the bar? During the melee, Don went in the store and stole Black Tone's coke stash, just to be trifling.

After the crowd dispersed, Lee, Reg, and TC went to the park side of 139th and Lenox with Black Tone staying in front of the bar. Lee wasn't done yet; he was even angrier now because Black Tone was able to get the best of Don with only an arm and a half. Lee kept yelling, "You ready to fight, nigga?!" from across the street.

Black Tone hollered, "I'm not fighting you, Lee."

"Ima let you catch your breath and get yourself together, cuz you fightin today, mf!" Lee continued.

Tone repeated himself.

Unbeknownst to everyone, Black Tone had sent his girl to get his gun after the commotion. He kept to the bar side of 139th St. while Lee was going back and forth with Reg and TC. They were trying to get him to stop the bullshit but Lee wasn't having that shit and kept going. He was so busy in his rant, Lee didn't notice Black Tone was now standing in the street. TC tapped Reg and said, "Yo, he got his thing on him."

Reg asked, "How u know?"

"That nigga stayed across the street this whole time. That mf is in the middle of the street now. He want Lee to keep it up. He gon pop him, watch." TC replied. Reg just shook his head because he could see where this was going. He walked in the street where Tone was standing and tried to reason with him.

Black Tone gave him a look, then said, "I'm good. You better tell that mf to chill the fuck out."

Lee never noticed Tone leave the corner, go into the bar and get his hammer, all because he was so busy talking shit. He never paid it any attention and it was too late now. TC told Lee, "That mf is gonna fire on you."

Why did he say that? It was like adding lighter fluid to a BBQ grill. Lee practically ran off the sidewalk into the street toward Black Tone yelling, "That faggot mf ain't gon do shit! You went and got your joint?! You better use it, mf!"

TC was right at Lee's side as he approached Black Tone so he could jump between them if need be. At this point, Tone was standing sideways with his hand in his pocket. Lee, still the aggressor, was trying to get at Black Tone. As he reached over Reg and TC one more time, Reg lost his balance and fell. Black Tone had enough; only TC stood between them now. The gun came out as Black Tone pushed TC out of his way to create a clear path to Lee. TC, seeing the gun, reached for Black Tone's arm but it was too late. When Lee saw it, he backed up saying, "Aight Tone. You got it. You got it, mf!"

Tone said, "No mf, *you* got it!" and pulled the trigger striking Lee in the leg. Blaow! His six foot plus, two hundred pound frame hit the ground like a fallen oak tree. Tone fired again, hitting him again in the same leg. Blaow!

Lee was on the ground yelling up at Black Tone, "Aight Tone, you shot me, you shot me! You got it! You got it!"

Black Tone stood over Lee, pointing the gun at his head this time and pulled the trigger, saying, "Ima kill you, mf!"

Click! Nothing happened. Lee was on the ground with his arms blocking his face, trying to squirm away from the line of fire. Black Tone pulled the trigger again. Click. Nothing. Again. Click. Same result. The gun was jammed. At this point, Tone had blacked out. Lee's baby's mother shouted, "What the fuck you doing?!"

Pointing the gun at her, he said, "Back the fuck up before I pop you too, bitch!"

Tone even spun around and pointed the gun at TC, who had to remind him who he was. He said, "Tone, it's me, my nigga! It's me!" Black Tone turned and walked around the corner. TC turned his attention to Lee who was still on the ground bleeding.

TC urged Lee to get up. He said, "I can't T, my leg, my leg!" TC picked Lee up from the ground, carrying him to the corner where a cab happened to be sitting at a red light. TC placed him in the back seat, shutting the door as the light turned green, and the driver headed off toward Harlem Hospital.

Black Tone was still in a rage. By now, he was in the passenger seat of his car as his chick is driving. Tone was f'n with the gun and finally dislodged the jammed bullet. As he looked up, Tone noticed the cab Lee was in headed downtown toward the hospital and he told his chick to pull alongside it. She asked, "What the fuck you gonna do?!"

"Just do what the fuck I told you to do," he barked. As instructed, she threw the u-turn, caught up to the cab at the next light and pulled up alongside. When Tone went to shoot into the cab, he saw his brother, Bill, in the backseat with Lee. Apparently the cab had picked him up before leaving the block. Tone immediately lowered the gun and told her to pull off so they could get the fuck out of there.

I don't know if you see things the way I do, but I would say God was with Lee twice that day.

Back at the block, everyone was in shock. In all our years growing up, no one had ever shot another. We had fights as kids but nothing as impetuous as that; women and kids were crying in the street. Black Tone's nephew sobbed, "My Uncle Tony shot my Uncle Lee."

That whole situation was crazy. More importantly, it was unnecessary and uncalled for. Our block was like a family and we were too close for shit like that. Our unity was the strongest part of our armor; to the outside, it now looked like there were chinks. Even amidst the bullshit, niggas still loved and cared for one another.

A week or so before this, Big L was in the gambling spot on Lenox owned by Bo. He happened to be losing this night and was sore about it. TC's god brother, Fella, was also in the spot. L got mad and threatened to punch him in the face for no reason other than being mad because he'd lost all his money. TC just watched to see if Fella was going to stand up and be a man. He didn't say anything but he gave his god brother the look as if to say, *if you let this mf put his hands on you, Ima put MY hands on you*. He didn't want that. That nigga
105

TC was f'n heavy-handed. Sure enough, Big L goes around the table and swings on Fella and they got to shaking. Big L was on the losing end of this one. After it'd broken up, he ran out of the spot to tell his brother. Lee went to the gambling spot, threatened niggas, found Bo's coke stash and took it.

Now, I'm not the smartest mf in the world; I'm just a black boy from 139th St. and I don't know everything. But what the fuck did Bo and his coke have to with L's one-on-one fight in the spot? The answer is NOTHING. L didn't get jumped; he didn't get robbed. So what the hell did Lee need to take the coke for? Lee didn't like Bo. Why? I couldn't tell you. I can only speculate it might have been because Bo had more money than him. Bo had a ten-year advantage on us in the game. He *should've* had more money! If he didn't, he was damn fool. (And a fool he was not.) Maybe it was because Bo had a gambling spot and Lee wanted one, who knows.

At any rate, the next day, Reg was sitting on the stoop of Building 108. Lee came down the block and said, "Where your man at? Ima punch him in his mouth when I see him."

"Who?"

"You know who," demanded Lee. Reg had already heard but he asked what happened anyway. "TC told Fella that he better fuck L up in the gambling spot last night," Lee clarified.

Reg just looked at him for minute with the *'Is this nigga really this stupid'* face, before questioning, "What the fuck did you expect him say? That's his god brother, Lee. Fuck you mad about that for? They fought one-on-one. What's the problem? If you was there you would've told L the same shit, right?"

Lee was incredulous, "I don't give a fuck. Ima punch that nigga n his mouth!"

"Well you go right ahead hit that nigga if you want to. You know him and you know that ain't gon turn out good," Reg reminded him.

TC just happened to be coming from around the corner and walked up to his building next to where they were standing. He said, "What's up Reg? What's up, asshole?" before walking into the building.

Always a clown, Reg started laughing. Now, if Lee really wanted some shit with TC, that would've been the perfect opportunity, but Lee wasn't f'n with him. He wanted no parts of those hands. That's how life was for us; the mf you claimed you wanted to hit in the mouth a week prior, is the same mf who picked your big ass up from the ground and carried you to a cab after you got shot. Some ironic shit, huh?

Lee didn't realize what he had. He was blinded by narcissism; a cloud that overshadowed his sensibility. Niggas really loved Lee and would've walked through fire for him. The loyalty niggas had for him was undeniable, but we were only his "homeboys."

Here's another example of how niggas rode for him..

In the early to mid-90's, there was wave of carjacking and stolen vehicles all over the country. It was so bad, that in 1992, Congress passed the Federal Anti-Car Theft Act (FACTA), making it a federal crime (punishable by fifteen years to life imprisonment) to use a firearm to steal "through force or intimidation" a motor vehicle that has been shipped through interstate commerce. In 1995, there was also a movie about the enormous amount of car thefts that took

107

place in and around Newark, NJ called, "New Jersey Drive". Guys would steal cars and take them for joyrides. Then someone found a way to capitalize off these kids by paying for the stolen vehicles, re-tagging them, (switching the VIN plates) and reselling them for an inflated price. This was big business back then. You would see a nigga who was barely in the game one day driving an $80,000 car the next, and think, *"How the fuck did he do that?"* The car was probably tagged. Niggas were popping up with all kinds of shit and they were being snatched out of those mfs by the police too.

Still, some took their chances; Lee being one of them. He paid $5,000 for a blue Mazda MPV. Back then, those were some hot joints! Remember, Jace Biggs had a white one. It almost made me jump out the window and cop one myself but for some reason, I didn't. Lee threw some chrome shoes (rims) on it so his shit would stand out.

Lee had his MPV for about a week or so and was loving it. One morning he comes outside and the van is gone. *I know I parked this mf right here*, he thinks to himself. He immediately called his kids' mother; she's the only other person who could've moved it. But it couldn't have been her; she hadn't left the house yet. So what the fuck happened? Lee was sick. Shit, I would've been too. There was no broken glass on the ground, so he wondered how the fuck the car got stolen. Good question.

It turns out the car wasn't stolen, exactly. The guy who sold Lee the car had kept an extra key and on the previous night he'd taken the parked car off the street from Lee and resold it to another person. How did he find that out? After the van was missing for about a week Lee got a call from someone who was at Olympic Diner on the Grand Concourse and 149th. They said his van was a couple of doors down at the gas station. Niggas were just chilling on the block when Lee got the call. He said, "Nigga just saw my joint! It's right across the bridge!" With no hesitation, we ran in my crib, grabbed them hammers, loaded up in a line of cars and flew across the bridge. When we got to the gas station, the van was still there. Whoever spotted dude basically stalled him until we showed up. That mf knew there was something fishy about the MPV, which is probably why he didn't resist. Think about it, if you bought a car legit, are you going to let a random mf stop you from getting in your shit and driving away? Hell mf, no! I know I wouldn't. I would've run his ass the fuck over! Anyway, we pulled up in the cars filled with niggas and guns. We blocked both driveways so no one could go in or out. All of us jumped out, hammers in hands, surrounding the dude and the van. The gas station attendant was paralyzed with fear. He couldn't get himself together to even try to call the police. People were jumping back in their cars and ducking down out of sight. They didn't want to see shit, or be seen.

Lee asked the dude, "Yo, where you get this van from?" As he tried to reply, Lee exclaimed, "Fuck all that! That's my mf'n shit. You stole it!"

Dude said, "But I bought this from so and so (I never got his name). I didn't steal it."

Lee went on, "Yeah, you bought it? How much you paid for those rims?"

Dude said, "I don't know, they were on when I bought it."

Lee said, "I know you don't know how much they cost because I put them shits on there! That's my shit!"

109

The dude tried to put up a good argument but Lee wasn't having that. "Yo, I don't want no problem but I'm telling you I didn't steal your shit. I bought this," he maintained.

"Take that shit up wit him, 'cause this shit going wit us tonight!" Lee declared.

Dude looked around, saw all that hardware and knew he had no wins. That nigga tossed the keys to Lee like he was a valet, walked out of the gas station and didn't look back for shit. Lee hopped in the MPV, we hopped in the rides and headed back to the block. Lee parked his shit in the garage on 132nd and 7th after that. He wasn't playing any games about that MPV! I don't know how the fuck we didn't go to jail that night. That shit was crazy. It could've gone left real quick. What if dude had a strong crew and he called for backup? If they arrived and saw their man surrounded by all that firepower, it would've been like the shootout scene from the movie, "Heat".

We didn't give a fuck; it didn't stop us from riding with Lee. That's how we rolled back then. Jail, or even the possibility of dying, didn't stop us from protecting our own. That's what Lee had. The love and loyalty we had for one another was irrefutable. If only he saw it for what it really was. That unyielding bond insulated Lee from a lot of bullshit. Niggas knew it wouldn't be easy to get at him. If they did, retaliation would be swift.

While that worked for most people, it was a different story where The Lynch Mob was concerned. They didn't fuck with Lee out of love and respect for Reg and TC, to keep it one hundred. At this particular time, The Lynch Mob had much bigger problems than the likes of Lee. It turns out a federal indictment had dropped on them and the alphabet boys were coming quickly! Little did Jase know, three people from his crew were arrested in the fall of '94 and one of them was cooperating. These secret meetings with the authorities led to subsequent arrests of thirteen Lynch Mob members (including a female), in the summer of '95. I remember the feds driving all of Fatboy's cars down Lenox, honking the horns screaming out the windows, "We got 'em! We got Fatboy! We got The Lynch Mob! We got those mfs!" There were BMWs, Benzes, and all kinds of shit seized by the government being paraded through Harlem in a caravan, celebrating TLM's takedown.

Sad to say, but as strong as their crew was on the street, some of them turned on one another when shit got thick. I won't mention any names because they've already been dragged through the mud enough and it's not my intention to discredit anyone. However, I do tip my hat to those who stood up and truly respected the life they chose and the downside that comes with it. There are too many fair-weather criminals nowadays.

The testimony of those who told, led to the conviction of Jase and many other LM members. He was sentenced to thirty years in prison, thus ending the so-called reign of terror in Harlem, bringing a multi-million dollar crack and cocaine empire to the ground.

When I hear about crews being taken down by the feds, I often wonder how the investigation got started in the first place. In this case, TLM was noticed by C-11 (a joint NYPD/FBI Violent Drug Task Force) as a major cocaine and crack operation to be watched back in 1988. But it wasn't until '94 that the case was ultimately made against them.

While I don't know everything, it's my experience that the government will allow a mf to sell drugs all day long but when you start dropping bodies, they'll step in and shut shit down. That's what

I think happened to TLM; with the vast amounts of cocaine being distributed, coupled by the murders, the feds had what they needed to hit them with the RICO (Racketeer Influenced and Corrupt Organizations) Act. This statute allowed leaders or bosses to be charged with crimes they ordered others to act out, thereby closing a loophole which may have otherwise left them exempt from trial because they themselves didn't commit the crime, personally. Also, a person who commits at least two acts of racketeering (ex. drugs and murder) which contribute to the advancement of an enterprise within a ten year period may be prosecuted under RICO law. According to C-11, TLM fit the description of such an organization and felt they should be dismantled. So, off they went to serve their time in federal prisons across the country. But before getting deep into their bids, someone in their crew sent a kite home, saying the feds were asking questions about another crew in Harlem.

That crew was NFL. While they'd been checking us out a full year before, the investigation wouldn't begin until 1997. With the money being generated from the block and the alleged murders Reg was accused of, NFL found themselves in the crosshairs of C-11. The only difference was, NFL wasn't getting money as a unit, like TLM. We were all separate entities, not even being supplied by the same connect. We had nothing to do with one another, and the alleged bodies hadn't dropped at the order of any one person. The bloodshed had no connection to the drugs. But it didn't look that way from the outside; to the rest of the world, we looked like a unit being guided by Lee. I'd even heard people say NFL stood for "Niggaz for Leroy", and of course, I checked them for that.

This played right into Lee's hands. He was finally getting the attention he so desperately coveted, albeit from the wrong mfs. For as long as I can remember, he had aspirations of being in control of everyone around him. Lee wore a sense of entitlement, as if he sat at NFL's helm, and lusted to be recognized as our leader. He wanted to be revered by people in the street and it worked, for the most part, with two exceptions: one, Lee knew the truth. Reg was the one putting that work in the street, not him, and Reg's reputation preceded him.

This ate Lee up on the inside and he built a deep resentment toward Reg. Like I said, by no means was Lee soft but he just didn't live up to the hype his name had come to carry. Secondly, this esteem Lee placed upon himself was self-proclaimed. While this may have been the perception to the outside world, I'm letting it be known once and for all, there was no boss in NFL. Shit, we weren't even a f'n gang! The feds just made it seem that way to suit themselves. We only moved together when there was beef. Otherwise, we earned independently of one another. However, C-11 didn't see it that way. If you left it up to them, Lee would be at the top the pyramid, with Reg as his chief enforcer and the rest of us moving crack under his command. I don't think this was the kind of attention Lee had in mind. To me, it was a clear case of what Mama always said, "Be careful what you wish for." But it was too late. The boys were onto NFL.

It's a good thing it was a federal investigation and not the state, because the state will lock your ass up first and *hope* they have a strong enough case to hold you. The feds work the opposite, building their case and then snatching a mf up when they know they've got you. This bought NFL more time on the street as the government worked on their investigation. It didn't make sense to stop hustling. Shit, the best thing to do was make as much bread as you could and try to hide it. Every day you stepped outside could very well be your last day of freedom. After a while, when nothing happened, niggas resumed their day to day activities. Thinking back, they probably thought the warning was bullshit due to the source.

So many guys on the TLM case had proven themselves unreliable and couldn't be trusted. They didn't have loyalty amongst themselves, let alone with an outsider. But the warning was very real. NFL was being watched.

Halftime

It Was a Good Year

Summer of 1996 was upon us and it was a good time to be in Harlem. There's always an unofficial anthem that came out to take us through the warmest season of the year and there were many hot songs that year but one that sticks out in my mind was, 'Only You' by 112. It was a smooth-flowing joint out of the Bad Boy camp and was the group's debut single. Versace was the designer most people wore and talked about. That name stayed in rapper's lyrics, especially Biggie's. When niggas partied, they threw on the finest silks, linen and alligator shoes that money could buy. That was back in the day when I liked to party. I didn't drink or dance much (I was good for a two-step), so when I went out it was really just to get dressed up. I needed that change because I was always on the block with jeans and sneakers on; the parties were my escape. I miss those days, but enough about me.

That summer, D Ferg came up with a brilliant idea; he organized a bus trip for everyone in Harlem. Ferg reached out to all the crews about it and everyone agreed it would was a good thing for the hood. The destination was nearby Bear Mountain; only a forty-five minute drive from NYC, it's a 5,025 acre state park, west of the Hudson River in Rockland County with picnic groves, a swimming pool, open fields, and basketball courts. The courts were our main concern. With buses shuttling everyone from the Harlem State Office Building, the hood was on its way to the "First Annual Harlem Picnic." All the crews were there and damn near everyone in Harlem attended. Ferg even invited Diddy and I thought it was cool for him to show up. After all, he is from Harlem.

Now, 112 had a hot song that year, but the joint I remember everyone playing that day was, 'No Diggity' by Blackstreet. That shit was hot! People had a great time that day, either at the pool,

BBQ'ing, drinking, smoking, or whatever they were into. That afternoon, NFL and Same Gang had a basketball game. I don't remember the outcome but it was all in good fun. Overall, the day was beautiful. No beefs, no problems, no bullshit. That's how it was supposed to be.

Around that same time, Big L was having problems at Columbia. Frustration on both sides reached an all-time high. The label didn't know what to do with Big L, no matter how much they professed to believe in his talent. He grew tired of watching other artists' careers flourish while his seemed to be at a standstill. There was no bad blood. They were just at a stalemate and eventually Columbia dropped Big L from the label. His lyrical style was far too much for them and he was fed up with a lack of effort to try and grasp where he was coming from. It turned out to be a blessing in disguise.

When life hands you lemons, what do you do? Make lemonade. Always the hustler, Big L's entrepreneurial spirit took over. With NFL already throwing parties, he capitalized on that idea and used his popularity to do the same. Throwing a few functions of his own to generate funds helped him segue into the world of an independent recording artist. Being released from Columbia was the best thing that could've happened to him. Independent was the way to go; it allowed artists to break free from the restrictions major record labels tried to impose. There was so much more money to be made in the indie lane. Back then, for every five thousand singles, you could earn $9,000 for yourself. So if you sold forty thousand singles for instance, that was $72,000 in your pocket. Your pocket; the artist, not the label's. The majors would never allow an artist to profit like that. They're way too greedy and don't have enough control over the artist, be it by creative direction, image, lyrics, production, videos, you name it. Major record labels require all those things, so they're not too fond of artists going independent.

Leaving the constraints of Columbia behind, Big L's release was the push he needed to begin his independent journey.

Third Quarter

1997 was the pivotal year for NFL and everyone in 139th St. Our lives would be changed forever, starting with Lee's, as he caught a charge for gun possession. He'd been on his way home after midnight stopping at the store on the corner of 139th and 7th. Due to the late hour, he had to use the compartment on the turntable to get his order instead of going inside. As he approached the window, he noticed a cop car creeping up the block, knowing they were most likely on him. He couldn't run because his leg was still fucked up so the best thing he could do is try to ditch his hammer, but where?

Lee thinks fast as the cops jump out the car to search him. Deciding to turn his back to them, he slid the gun out of his waist, placed it in the compartment and spun it to the guy working in the store. The cops didn't see shit! *I'm good,* he thinks. Nope. The store clerk left the gun in the window and spun it back to Lee. He thought, *Ain't that about a bitch!* By this time, the cops were right up on him. With nowhere to run, even if he could, Lee took the charge. That was some real bullshit! The clerk could've kept the gun until the police left and passed it back to Lee later; it's not like he didn't know him. That was some sucker shit, but you can't be too mad at a civilian. He wanted no parts of the police.

So now Lee has an open case. Money had to be put up for bail, lawyers, and all kinds of shit all over again. Around this time, the relationship between Reg and Lee is kind of strained. To put my finger on it and say I know exactly why would be lying; but I will say it may have something to do with the fact that Reg was getting more notoriety in the street. His reputation was building momentum and it wasn't solely because his gun went off. Reg was a pleasure to be around. He didn't care for his dark side to be exposed and as long as he was respected, he was content.

Others wore their rep on their chest like a badge. They made it their business to throw their weight around and intimidate whoever was in their presence. It was displayed in the way they walked, talked, and how they dealt with people in general. Some niggas' egos were larger than their reps.

Reg was the opposite. Have you ever heard the expression "you can catch more flies with honey than with vinegar?" Well, I don't have to tell you which was which out of Reg and Lee. Having spent a considerable amount of time locked up in recent years, Reg had made some essential alliances. One of whom was a livewire from Queens named Nickelz.

The two had formed a bond that would stand strong, and brainstormed to get money upon release. Promising to keep in touch, their bond grew into a true friendship. If either had a lick, they'd notify the other so both could participate in the come up. Nickelz was fond of the party scene; not just for the music and chicks either. He knew all the players would be dressed to the nines, sporting Versace, gators and the like. But that wasn't his concern; niggas' shines were his focus. Dudes threw on their best jewels for these occasions: chains, rings, bracelets, watches, and of course, their money, were all on the menu, but especially the watches.

Iced-out Rolies were their favorites. Nickelz and Reg would dress up to blend in and attend these parties with the intent to catch a half drunk party-goer stumbling to his ride at the end of the night. But don't get it f'd up; while no one was exempt, a drunk mf was just easier. Once, after scoping a potential victim, Reg left the party a few minutes before it was over to get right. He went to the car, got his 9mm and wrapped it in a hand towel. Always making sure his driver was next to a garage, he would lie in wait. Reg saw a victim amongst the crowd as the venue emptied. As he was moving in for the kill,

121

Reg noticed a well- known Queens rapper wearing an iced-out chain and Rolex. Reg thought, *Oh, I'm gon get this mf!* Reg waited until the rapper walked past and headed down the ramp to get his car. He followed, and when close enough, Reg pulled the towel off the 9 and told the rapper not to move. The rapper spun around and when he saw that barrel in his face took off running, screaming bloody murder! Others in the garage took notice and began to scatter when they saw Reg with the ratchet. But that didn't stop him. He gave chase anyway, determined to catch his prey. The rapper proved to be too fast, making it all the way to the other side of the garage, running out into the street. There was no way Reg was going to catch him. Besides, he was trying to run in some slippery-ass gators. Even though that night was a bust for Reg, there were many that weren't. He and Nickelz had their share of triumphs.

Both men realized how thorough the other was, and how they could build together. A long lasting friendship was established and united, there was no stopping the two. This brings us to the summer of '97; that was another great one for me. It seems like when things are going well, something bad is never too far off.

D Ferg organized the 'Second Annual Harlem Picnic' to be held at Bear Mt. again. This time, instead of just Harlem, other boroughs were in attendance and the turnout was twice the size of the previous year. Ferg's industry connections and street cred enabled him to draw a much larger crowd. Among them was a Supreme Team stalwart named Colbert 'Black Just' Johnson. 'Just' was short for Justice, which was the Righteous name chosen by Colbert in order to become a true follower of the 5 Percent Nation. This was an Islamic sect started by Clarence 13X Smith when he defected from the Nation of Islam in 1963. The core belief he instilled in his followers was that the black man was God, or Supreme Beings. Almost everyone in the Supreme Team took a Righteous name. Headed by Kenneth "Supreme" McGriff, there was Gerald "Prince" Miller (Supreme's nephew and 2nd in command), and "Bimmy", another trusted and loyal brother, among many others.

In the 80's, Supreme ran a multi-million dollar crack and cocaine operation out of Baisley Projects in Queens. At their peak in 1987, their operation stretched out far beyond Baisley into other boroughs. Black Just, as he was commonly referred to, was a lieutenant in the organization, answering mainly to Supreme himself. Starting as a worker, he quickly rose in ranks until he ran a crew of his own. Black Just held the team down when members were locked up, simultaneously running the day to day operation of his own, earning him stripes and subsequently becoming one of Preme's favorites. He made frequent trips to visit Preme and relayed instructions to Prince. After Prince got picked up, Black Just and Bimmy stepped up to the plate and held the team down. Both having aspirations far beyond the streets, they delved heavily into the hip-hop scene and sought opportunities for the team to make that lucrative transition. Black Just hung out in Harlem sometimes with fellow hood celebrities like Rich and Flaco, and frequented clubs like Rooftop, Latin Quarter and The Tunnel with hip-hop stars and stars-to-be. He was well known and loved throughout NYC.

Both hailing from Queens, Black Just and Nickelz had a rapport. Each man had a mutual respect for the other. This made the introduction of Black Just and Reg at the Harlem Picnic possible. Black Just attended with a crew of Supreme Team subordinates and Reg was there with the entire NFL. The three men caught the attention of others, as they stood out from the crowd. It seemed like all eyes were on them, and they were. BJ had heard good things about Reg through Nickelz and now he could put a face to the name.

Afterward, Reg told TC how well the meeting went and how BJ intended to do for them what Rich and Flaco were going to do before all the bullshit went down. NFL was going to be flooded with work. He also said how BJ was going to help them make the transition from streets to music so he and Nickelz could put the guns down. And with Big L already in the game, it would've been beautiful.

The business part of the day was complete; now it was time to enjoy the festivities. The BBQ grills were going, people were at the pool, but most were sitting in folding chairs listening or dancing to music. The hottest song that summer was 'Put Your Hands Where My Eyes Can See' by Busta Rhymes. The bass line on that mf was so mean, you couldn't sit still! I don't care if you bobbed your head, tapped your feet, or snapped your fingers, something on your body was definitely going to be moving; the beat was that serious.

Basketball games were played and the crowd loved it; it was another good day for Harlem. Stopped at a service area to gas up on the way home, niggas just stood around kicking it. Lee, obviously feeling some kind of way, started saying slick shit pertaining to Reg chilling with Black Just, Nickelz and the Supreme Team niggas at the picnic. Things like, "That's Reg from Queens. Reg don't fuck with NFL no more, he's a Supreme Team nigga now." Or, he just referred to him as 'Queens Reg.' This was typical behavior for Lee. Reg basically ignored him. He wasn't trying to feed into Lee's ignorance. His mind was focused on the bigger picture, and how this connection with BJ was going to make shit better for the whole team. Even Lee's dumbass would've benefitted.

But Lee hated the fact that Reg could link up with someone of Black Just's caliber and he himself couldn't. Reg's welcoming personality had always been a gateway for opportunity, with things falling his lap. Lee, on the other hand, had an off-putting demeanor. He was unapproachable, so people generally kept their distance and he was cool with that. But Lee personally felt like he was NFL's leader; like he was 'The Man in Charge.'

Lee also hated the fact that Reg got more attention, more admiration, made more alliances, and therefore had the opportunity to make more money; potentially more than Lee. Now, I'm not saying he was jealous of Reg but what would you call it?

In my eyes, it was a classic case of the biblical Cain and Abel. If you don't know the story, here it is: Cain was the firstborn son of Adam and Eve, Abel being the younger brother. In those times, God required you to make sacrifices unto Him as a sign of appreciation. What you sacrificed showed God how grateful you were for all the blessings bestowed upon you. Cain was a farmer and grew fruits and vegetables for the family to eat. Abel was a shepherd with flocks of sheep that he tended to. One day God summoned them both to offer up a sacrifice on behalf of themselves. Cain gathered some produce and made his offering. Abel, on the other hand, found the VERY BEST of his flock; along with fatty pieces and sacrificed them to Him. While God's favor was shown to Abel and his offering because he sacrificed his very best, the opposite was shown to Cain because he basically threw some veggies together. This made the elder brother grow hot with anger. He invited Abel out the field, where they would be secluded. In a fit of jealous rage, Cain struck and killed Abel. Later, God asked Cain, "Where is your brother?" He replied with the infamous expression, "I do not know. Am I my brother's keeper?" God cursed Cain for killing Abel and banished him to walk the earth as a fugitive. That's how the story went.

Now, I'm not saying Lee would've gone as far as to kill Reg, but as we can see from Cain and Abel, a jealous mf is a dangerous

125

one, agreed? After all, Envy is one of the Seven Deadly Sins. Need I say more? Until the plans Black Just and Reg spoke about came to fruition, Reg had to eat. And of course, he did what he knew best. He had to go work. The gun was the tool of his trade and that trade was taking.

Whenever Reg saw a come up, he was on it. One day while sitting in the park he noticed a group of guys across the Ave chilling by Delano Houses and one of them wore a gold chain with a diamond encrusted cross. Reg moved closer to get a better look, noticing that it was Biggie's people from BK. They were uptown visiting a guy from Delano named Brandon who was cool with Diddy and worked security for him from time to time. There were a good half dozen of those mfs across the Ave but Reg didn't give a fuck. He was determined to get that chain. He sat back and waited for the perfect chance to make his move. He's doing all this while chilling with a bunch of niggas on the block. This nigga had the hammer on him and everything. They had no idea what he was up to. No one, except for TC. He always knew when Reg was on his bullshit. When Reg had his sights on a vic, he'd wait patiently to make his move. But he knew these niggas weren't going to be out for long, so he had to act soon. There were a lot of them and moving solo would've been risky but he was going if he had to. That chain was not making its way back to BK that day. Finally, he got the shot he needed. Biggie's man came across the street to the Chinese restaurant and he was solo. Reg thought, *I got this mf now!*

In the middle of the conversation Reg said, "I'll be back," and quickly left the group of guys he was chilling with. Reg casually walked into the spot while Biggie's man was placing his order. He had his back to the door and paid no attention when Reg came in. Reg hit him with a vicious shot to the body, doubling Biggie's man over in pain and shock. Customers stepped back and out of the way. Reg lifted his shirt, reached in his waist, pulled out the 9 and said, "You know what this is." Now, Biggie's man was a thorough mf himself, but at this point he didn't have much of a choice. He gave up the chain and left the restaurant. Reg walked to the curb and caught a cab around the corner to stash the chain at his girl's crib. Reg called TC and told him to meet him on the corner of the block with his hammer. He walked back to the park and watched Biggie's man and the rest of the niggas across the street. Brandon was looking across the Ave to see who was over on our side and noticed it was Reg and TC. TC stashed the hammer and listened as Reg filled him in on what just transpired. TC said, "I knew yo ass was on some bullshit."

As Reg and TC stood on the block watching the niggas across the Ave, Brandon made his way across to talk to them. He said, "Reg, can I talk to you for a min?" Now, Brandon was a big mf. Like I said, he did security for Diddy. Reg was around six feet tall, but he only weighed about 170lbs.

"What the fuck you want?" Reg asked.

"Yo, that chain you took was my man's. I need that back, my nigga," Brandon requested.

Reg said, "Get the fuck outta here! I ain't giving shit back!"

"Come on Reg, those are my people. Don't do it like that, my nigga," Brandon implored.

Reg said, "You know how this shit goes. If I got caught slipping out in BK you think them niggas woulda gave me my shit back? Hell no! So don't come over here asking to give shit back! Tell him to get in blood!"

127

Brandon looked at TC and asked, "Yo T, can you talk to him?"

TC said, "You heard what the man said."

With that, Brandon just turned and walked away.

When niggas told me what happened, I couldn't believe it. TC told me it was the same chain Biggie wore on an episode of "Martin". I couldn't' wait to see that episode. I had to see for myself. Sure enough, there the chain was, around Biggie's neck. Now, I don't know if it was the same one Reg took from his man, but the chain and cross Reg had looked exactly like the one BIG wore on that show. So I just put two and two together, shook my head and said to myself, *this nigga Reg is off the hook.*

Oh well, that's how the game goes. I respect it but I'll never accept it. Things around 139th moved at its normal daily pace. Lee still had the park shaking while fighting his gun case. TC was doing his one-two step here and there, but nothing like before. Basically he was just doing what he needed to survive.

He was really trying to step away from the game altogether to concentrate on his artwork. TC had a plethora of ideas and being frustrated with the streets at that time, he decided to focus his attention in that direction. Black Tone was still getting money but it was never the same since he wasn't coming around the block after shooting Lee. Reg, Gee, and his cronies were always on the lookout for the next lick. There were lean times and frustrating at that, with Reg's money getting low. When a nigga like him gets desperate, things can get hairy.

He was doing his best to provide for his family, but shit wasn't going well. His daughter suffered from sickle cell anemia and

128

she needed medication. Reg had to do something quick. He couldn't borrow it from Black Tone and TC had one foot out of the game, so his money was tight. His relationship with Lee was almost nonexistent, so that was a no go. He couldn't go to Gee. Gee ate whenever he did, so they were in the same boat. Although he didn't want to, he pawned the chain to get the meds for his baby girl. Now it was back to square one and Reg was on the hunt for the next come up. He reached out to Nickelz for direction, but came up short. Reg knew the game and realized it wouldn't be the last time he would need to pawn that chain. He had to get that shit back because it was his ace in the whole for despondent situations. I don't know what fell in his lap, or what jux he came up on, but he did manage to get the chain out of hock.

Lee and Reg's relationship was already strained but when Lee saw that he finally got the chain back, he stopped speaking to Reg completely. Reg brought it to TC's attention and all he could do was shake his head with a little laugh. That shit was crazy. Although I never witnessed that myself, I know for a fact Lee stopped speaking to me when I was getting money up the block.

From 1994 to 1997, I was Lee's main competition in 139th St. He had his situation down in the park and I had mine. We'd established boundaries and both parties honored them. At some point, my clientele began to either match or even surpass his, or so it seemed. I would never know for sure what his numbers were, but it didn't matter. My only concern was my building. Somehow, the fact that it appeared like I was getting money irritated him because he stopped speaking to me. Notice, I didn't say I was getting *more* money, just money.

Keep in mind, Lee had been doing numbers in the park for years by this time. He had a nice run. A NICE ONE! During this

129

time, niggas around him had hits and misses when it came to paper and he was fine with that. He was content to get money in the park while the same niggas who would risk life and freedom for him got scraps. The crazy shit was, those same niggas were fine with it as well. Our mentality was, Lee came home, turned up, and built his empire. He worked for it, so he deserved it. But why was it a problem for someone else in the block to achieve similar success? It was fine when he did it. For that question, I offer no answer. All I know is, that man walked past me in silence like I was a fire hydrant on a daily basis. (We never spoke again.) I was baffled, but not as much as when I heard he wasn't f'n with Reg because of the chain.

Lee and I were always cool and I loved him like all my NFL brothers, but we never had the bond he shared with Reg. They had triumphant highs, disappointing lows, and through it all they held each other down. I was extremely confused as to how their relationship had deteriorated to that extent. Never will I understand how a man envies another man. That was Lee just being Lee. By then, we were used to him and his ways, but no one could've foreseen this.

If there was ever a time that made TC and Reg look at Lee in a different light, it was this next instance. Whenever it was that Lee found it in his heart to speak to Reg again, they resumed a cordial relationship. One average day around the block, Reg and TC were chilling in the park. Lee was still fighting his gun case at that point and was returning from court. He casually approached them and said the most peculiar thing. Now, before I go further I want to put this out there: he may have uttered these words in jest, but where we come from, you don't play like that.

After exchanging the normal pleasantries, Lee said, "Guess what the DA told me." That was strange right out the gate, but they continued listening. He continued, "He said he'll cut me a deal if I give you two niggas up."

Reg got annoyed instantly and replied, "Fuck you *mean* he'll cut you a *deal*?! You snitchin, mf?"

Lee jumped on that, "Fuck you, nigga! Ain't nobody tellin! Fuck outta here!"

"So what the fuck you say that dumb shit for?" TC asked.

"Fuck both y'all niggas!" and Lee walked off.

This really had their minds racing. What the hell was wrong with this nigga, Lee? Now, I don't know about you, but I've had my share of run-ins with the court system and not once has a DA ever, *ever* talked to me directly. My attorney never came to me with any type of bullshit like that. I would've been insulted if they did.

Knowing Lee the way I know him, he should've been too. So why would he say that? And even if he was joking, why would he play with those two mfs like that? They all had dirt on each other and could definitely be used as a bargaining tool to swing the pendulum of justice their way if properly massaged. Whatever the motive, playing or not, Reg and TC didn't take that shit lightly. They knew they had to keep an eye on him from then on.

The Turning Point

Around 1989, right before he was about to start his bid for the armed robbery, Lee met one of his cousins on his father's side of the family. Lee went to Richman High School with another cousin, who, for whatever reason, he didn't particularly care for. But this other cousin was getting money, so I guess he was more suited to Lee's fancy. After meeting this cousin, they became cool although I wouldn't say go so far as to say they were close. Both men respected the other and remained amiable.

The cousin had his coke thing going on The Hill and Lee had his thing in the block. Lee went away to do his bid and that was that. Fast forward to 1997, the year Reg turned thirty years old. I remember as clear as day, him saying to me, "I made it, Lou! I made it to thirty!" It's sad, but our life expectancy was very low back then. Living to see thirty was an accomplishment, especially the way Reg was living. I didn't think I would make it out of my twenties either. I stayed in some shit back then. But Reg made it, and it felt good.

Shortly after Reg's birthday, tragedy struck once again in the worst way. Lee's new-found cousin was shot and killed on the way into his building. (RIP to him and condolences to his family and loved ones.) I remember when I got the call the next day. I was driving downtown on 8th Ave by 132nd St. and slammed on the brakes. I had to pull over to get out of the car; I was too f'd up to continue driving. When I got myself together, I turned the car around and went uptown where Lee's cousin hustled. I needed confirmation. When I got there all of his people were in tears so I knew it was true. I couldn't believe it. He was a super cool dude. Niggas everywhere were devastated, to say the least. I couldn't wrap my head around it. No one knows every move a nigga makes or who they may have a problem with, but I never knew Lee's cousin to beef with anyone. To my knowledge, all he did was make money and take care of his family. It's sad what the streets do to us; what we do to ourselves, to be more accurate.

Just like every other homicide, the theories started spreading fast with everyone speculating. One theory had his long-time on-again off-again girlfriend conspiring with her new man to have him murdered for insurance money. If I'm not mistaken, the two of them were picked up and questioned for it. The most popular hypothesis would have Reg as the shooter. Why? I don't know. Maybe it's because at the time of the shooting, it was reported that the killer (or killers) rode up to the victim on a motorcycle and shot him. (At the time, Reg had been riding one in the days leading up to the murder.) Now, this could've been a crazy coincidence. Or, Reg could've been one hundred percent responsible. Only the parties involved know the facts.

The news spread through the hood like a wildfire and of course, Lee got the wire. I can't say for sure, but he was probably f'd up by it. He never had the chance to build a solid relationship with his cousin. Not that they were working toward it, but now they couldn't even if they'd wanted to. With the rumor of him being the culprit flying around, it made Reg a marked man.

Lee's cousin had been loved by many, so there was a long list of those who may have wanted retribution for his death. Reg became aware of this fact and he still went about his daily life as if everything were the same. But life wasn't the same for Lee.

I'm not the smartest person in the world, but if I thought my man was responsible for the death of my cousin, I would've approached him about it. You know, give him a chance to clear his name with me. That would also give me a chance to get a read on his vibe. A lot of times, mfs will give themselves away without knowing. However, Lee did nothing resembling that.

In true Lee fashion, he stopped fucking with Reg again, putting a heavy burden on an already strained relationship. Reg looked at it as Lee just being Lee, and kept it moving. In his mind, a pot of revenge was brewing like coffee on a Monday morning. Somehow, some way, he was going to make Reg pay.

In the street, there's no better satisfaction than an eye for an eye. In his mind, Reg had to pay with his life. After his cousin's burial, Lee put his plan into motion, beginning to devise an unsavory scheme to execute one of his closest friends. Knowing his name was buzzing about the motorcycle hit, Reg played the block a lot closer. He wasn't trying to get caught slipping, so home base was the way to play it safe. This made it more difficult to hit him outside the block. Reg's kids' mother and their children moved to the Eastside close to 118th St. It was a quiet block without much activity, especially at night. Although no longer in a relationship, he cared for her and his children very much. Everyone knew how Reg felt about his kids. He went all out for anybody he loved, so imagine how he felt about his own offspring.

One night, Reg received a series of beeps from his baby mother's number with the 911 code attached. Everyone knows what that 911 code meant back in the day, especially if it came from your wife, girl, baby mama, or your niggas. Drop everything, and get yourself to a payphone, or wherever you needed to be to make sure shit was alright! But for some reason, when Reg got those beeps, he didn't rush across town. He called first instead. When his bm picked up, he asked what was wrong. Her response was, "What are you talking about?"

Reg said. "You beeped me 911. What's wrong?"

"I don't know what you're talking about, Reggie. I didn't beep you," she replied.

Reg found that strange and brushed it off for the moment. It happened again on another night; same tactic, same result. Shit wasn't making sense. But with no evidence of the source of the beeps, what could he do but be extra cautious?

Getting rid of Reg wasn't easy but the conspirators were determined. Where there's a will, there's a way. On Sept 21st, Reg was chilling on the corner of 139th and Lenox like he typically did. The Tunnel, a popular club in the 80's and 90's jumped on Sundays when they catered to the hip-hop crowd. Big L went to Reg and asked if he could borrow his chain to wear to the club that night. I wasn't around, but had I been, it would've made me think twice. *Why would L need to borrow Reg's chain when he already has his own jewelry?*

Reg thought nothing of it and gave Big L the chain. The next night however, I know Reg found it peculiar when Big L asked for the chain again. With little fuss, he relented. Minutes after L retrieved the jewelry, an unmasked gunman approached Reg as he was leaning back on a parked car and fired four or five rounds into his chest. Blaow! Blaow! Blaow! Blaow! Reg's slim six foot frame fell to the ground as the people around him scrambled to get to safety. Lee and a couple of his cronies were standing a few buildings up the block when the shots rang out. Immediately, he and his people jumped in the MPV and backed down the block where Reg laid, clinging to his last bit of life. They lifted Reg's body into the van and drove to Harlem Hospital. Upon arrival, they carried Reg into the emergency room where the staff began the process of trying to save what was

135

left of his existence. It was to no avail. Despite their efforts he could not be revived.

Forty days after his 30th birthday, Reg was dead. The news spread quickly. Crowds began to gather at the hospital as people consoled one another in disbelief. The whole block was in shock. I was home in bed when I got the call from my man, Bum, and I couldn't believe my ears. I had to make sure. Immediately, I called Reg's mother's house. As soon as the call connected, I knew it was true. All I heard was uncontrollable screaming and crying in the background. I asked to speak to his sister but she couldn't get herself together enough to come to the phone.

I was f'd up. My girl and I jumped in a cab and went to the hospital where a crowd had formed. With significant police presence also there, I was being extra cautious because I was on the run from a drug case I caught a year earlier. My girl (who I later married) and Reg's girl were good friends. When we walked in, the hospital staff was just about to let Reg's girl go in the room to see his body. She asked if I would go in with her so I took her by the arm and we walked to the room where Reg was lying on the table. He was stitched from his abdomen up to his chest, his eyes slightly open so you could see a small amount of the whites. Surprisingly, his girl remained calm while looking at him lying there. I believe she was in shock more than anything. Me, I was beyond numb. It was all too surreal. The thought of one of us being dead was unfathomable. But, there he lied, right before me.

To this day, nineteen years later, at the time of this writing, I still can't believe it. Reg's death was the inception of NFL's downfall; he had been the glue that held us together. Like I've said, everyone knew Reg had enemies; but niggas were stuck trying to figure out where the shit came from. Whenever a mf gets hit in the hood, the first thing one thinks is that it came from the inside. The finger automatically points to the closest person to the victim and works its way outward.

The rumors started to swirl. It came from his past. It was Lee. Someone even said Gee had something to do with it but that shit didn't make any sense. Reg and Lee had their differences, but to actually have him killed was too far out there. The Gee theory was delivered to Reg's family as a deflection. That shit was ludicrous to us and it soon dissipated.

It had to be something from his past that came back to haunt him; what else could it be? Reg had done a lot of shit, so narrowing it down wasn't going to be easy. His family was completely devastated. With rumors about Gee and Lee being responsible, they didn't know who to trust. When Gee heard the news he was so grief-stricken, he broke down three times and had to be picked up from the ground. His mentor, best friend, and brother was gone.

Gee was lost. Reg's death created a fire in him that burned like an inferno. There was no way mfs would get away with this! Somebody was going to pay! The only question was, who? Niggas had homework to do, but first things, first.

The family had to lay Reg to rest. His service was held a few days later at Riverton Funeral Home. The wake was without incident. The funeral however, was a different story. Still on the run, I decided not to attend the funeral. I hadn't really left the house much after Reg was killed but I had to see my fallen brother one more time. I stepped into the service quickly to view his body and left immediately. Approaching the casket, I noticed Reg was wearing a multi-colored Versace shirt and some black slacks. Draped around his neck, lying on his chest, was the gold chain and cross. I touched

Reg's hand, told him I loved him and kissed him on the cheek. It cut me to my heart to know I would never see my NFL brother again. I turned and quickly walked out of the funeral home. Although I didn't see this myself, I was later told Lee and his people wore Versace shirts, slacks and gators, like Reg. It was almost as if they were dressed for a party.

Was this a celebration the rest of us didn't know about? If that's what niggas were going to wear to send our brother off, shouldn't the entire NFL family have received the memo? It seemed like Lee was trying to create a division and in a way, he did. That display at the funeral showed everyone who his people were and who's side they chose. Lee only notified who he wanted dressed that way, a decision made collectively amongst themselves.

The other thing was a flower arrangement designed in the shape of a motorcycle. Maybe outwardly there wasn't anything peculiar about that; it was common knowledge that Reg had loved riding them, but was it a subliminal message from Lee to taunt Reg, acknowledging the fact that he knew Reg had killed his cousin while riding a bike? Maybe it was a coincidence, maybe not.

Afterward, everyone made their way to their cars to escort Reg to his final resting place. The funeral procession was a decent size, as Reg was well loved. Arriving at the cemetery in NJ, everyone said their goodbyes and bid Reg farewell.

We love you, comrade.

Our beloved son, brother, and father.

You fell on this earth, but rose to the heavens above.

Gone but never forgotten.

Forever in our hearts.

Matthew "Reggie" White

1967-1997

NFL Forever

When people grieve, they sometimes think irrationally; but now was the time for niggas to do some real homework. One of ours was taken. This had never happened to us before and mfs were in shock. I can't lie, I was f'd up for a good minute. I had seen many dead bodies in my life and heard of countless murders, but none affected me like this. When it's close to home, it's a totally different ball game.

Now attempting to narrow down the suspects starting from the closest outward, it was Gee and another guy from the block who shall remain nameless. They were eliminated as possibilities immediately because there was no motive, no beefs, and no problems whatsoever, and the two of them would've killed for Reg; that's how deep the love and loyalty ran with them. If you worked outward, the focus turned to TC. Once again, no problems there. TC was eliminated. Next in line would be Lee. Why would Lee want Reg dead? Disagreements arose here and there, but was it enough to kill the other? I think not. What about Lee's cousin and the fact that the streets were saying Reg was responsible? That's kind of deep. That was definitely a strong enough motive to move on Reg, or was it? Remember, Lee gave TC and Reg the green light to kill his cousin, Country, back in the day. Country and Lee had grown up together, as opposed to the new cousin he met around 1989. Who's to say Lee loved one more than the other? I can only speak for myself when I say I would ride for family I knew all my life before I rode for family I just met a few years prior. Maybe it's just me.

I know up to now I've pointed the finger at Lee and made him look like the culprit and for that I'm wrong. But let's look a little deeper at Reg's murder.

There's a story circulating on the internet stating Reg's killer was instructed to blast the guy wearing the gold chain. I often wondered how that small, but key bit of information could've gotten leaked to the public except from a co-conspirator. But, I'm no Sherlock Holmes; what do I know?

On the contrary; the night he was killed, Big L didn't place the chain around Reg's neck. Instead, he'd asked to borrow the chain again just as he'd done, the previous night. But it was a Monday. What the hell did L need the chain for on a Monday night? TC even asked him why he let L hold it the first night but Reg told him it was cool and that he shouldn't sweat it. But shit didn't sit right with TC. He remembered how shady Lee had acted when Reg got the chain out of the pawn shop. If he was there the night Reg was hit, he would've looked at Reg like he was crazy for giving it to Big L again. But no one was there to protest, so Reg gave it up.

Witnesses said Reg's shooter was a tall, light-skinned guy who walked right up to him. Reg was no dummy; he knew his name was being stirred in the pot as a suspect in Lee's cousin's murder, as well as other shit he did. He was always on point. With his lifestyle, he had to be. But Reg was definitely on high alert at that time, because the murder of Lee's cousin was still fresh. Allowing someone to casually walk up to him was way out of Reg's character; he wouldn't have permitted it. But what if the shooter was familiar to Reg? Maybe he recognized the shooter and didn't pay him any mind because it was someone he knew.

It just so happens, Lee had been seen on the block with a guy who fit the description of Reg's alleged killer. (This was a common tactic of Lee's. He would align himself with outside shooters, or so called thugs, and bring them around the block to intimidate his own people.) It made no sense, but again, that was Lee being Lee. Once, TC even asked Reg who the dude was that was hanging out with Lee. Reg replied, "Someone who's gonna get his head blown off if he acts up." How ironic. Was it a coincidence that Lee's man fit the description? Maybe so. What about the events after Reg got shot? Lee and his people had been standing a few buildings away from the scene. After the shooting they jumped in his MPV and backed it down to Lenox, loaded Reg into the van and drove up to 7th Ave. Now if your friend was bleeding to death, wouldn't it make sense to back the vehicle out of the block onto Lenox so you could get to Harlem Hospital quicker? They were already close to Lenox anyway! I'm not a rocket scientist, but that's what I would've done. Then they waited for the light to turn green once they reached 7th Ave. Why the fuck would you do that?! Lee was a mf'n criminal since he was a f'n teenager. You mean to tell me he was afraid to run a red light when he had a dying man in his car?! What's the worst thing that could've happened, a traffic ticket? Under those circumstances, I would think the points on his license were worth it. But, wait there's more.

People who were on the block when the shooting occurred walked the three blocks to Harlem Hospital's ER and arrived before Lee did, and he was driving! How was that even possible?! Was Lee really trying to save the life of his one-time friend? I'll let you, the reader, form your own opinion. Once these facts started to surface, Lee was looking more and more like a fox in a hen house with blood on its chin. The thought of killing one of our own was unimaginable. When I heard Lee may have been responsible, my heart was broken even more. What the fuck had become of us? How could we fall to the depths of deceit and betrayal to the point of murdering one another? Not us. Not NFL. And not those two, of all people. That was like Michael Jordan killing Scottie Pippen. The more I heard, the more I despised that block and everything about it. I never looked at people the same again. EVER.

The rumors were starting to eat at Lee. The night of Reg's wake, TC, Unc , and White Tone were chilling in the park when Lee's right hand man, a dangerous mf approached TC and asked him where Gee was. Everyone knew Lee's man from when we were younger; he was from the block, but he had just returned from doing a ten year stretch (but before he left, the nigga was deadly with a handgun). He was nothing to be f'd with. TC asked him, "Why, what's up?"

Standing in front of TC with black gloves on, he replied, "That mf is going around tellin people my brother murdered Reg!"

TC shook his head, stood up and giving a sarcastic smile, he replied, "First of all, my brother is dealing with emotions right now and there's no tellin what he might be saying. Second, I don't give a fuck what he said, ain't nobody doin a mf'n thing to him!"

As he said this, TC took his watch off and handed it to Whitey. Unc stood up and turned to the side so he could get good leverage in case he had to crack that mf. But TC gave Unc a look as if to say, *I got him. Ima knock this nigga the fuck out!* But Lee's man didn't bite. He just turned and left the park. All of this took place while Lee was standing outside the park but within earshot. TC said his piece and walked out of the park past him as Lee asked if he could talk to him. TC couldn't possibly figure out what he would have to say after all this time, because they hadn't really f'd with each other in a good minute. But TC stopped to hear him out.

Lee said, "I know we haven't been the best of friends lately, but we're the last two real mfs left. When I find out who did this shit to Reg, we gon handle it, me and you."

TC looked at him and thought, *this nigga must think I screw my head off and put it on the nightstand at night.* Extending his hand for Lee to shake it, he looked him dead in the face and said, "No doubt, homeboy. Just let me know." Then he walked off. In the back of his mind he knew Lee was guilty. There was just no way to prove it.

Lee had to feel some sort of way after that exchange, especially after TC called him homeboy. His own subliminal was thrown back in his face. He knew TC felt some kind of way because of the "homeboy" remark. Lee was no dummy; he knew he had to keep an eye on TC after that. But TC was not the most pressing situation he had to deal with. If the streets felt he was guilty of Reg's murder, eventually the police would get wind of it as well, and he couldn't have that. To make matters worse, he still had his gun case to fight.

The weeks following Reg's death had the block in limbo. Everyone was trying to recover and TC was trying to put pieces together, but his head was still spinning. Gee walked around in a daze. On one of those occasions when TC went to check on Reg's mother, he walked in and saw Lee sitting on Reg's bed with his arm around her, telling her how he was going make what happened to her son, right. After hearing that, TC turned and walked out. Reg's mother called to him, asking what was wrong but TC left the house thinking, *this nigga is f'n Bishop!* He couldn't help but shed a tear, wondering, *what the fuck had become of my brothers? How could we have sunk so low?*

Things around 139th St would never be the same but niggas had to press on. Life had to continue. Reg would've wanted it that way. Lee's case was coming down to the wire. He was either going to trial or taking a plea. Ultimately, he copped to a determinate sentence of five years and was given a sentence date to start doing his time. Now he had the task of getting his affairs in order before his departure; that's not a good feeling. Trust me, I know. I've been there more times than I'd like to admit.

While awaiting sentencing, Lee did something rather unusual, he went to Reg's family and asked for his death certificate. Lee went on to explain that he wanted to show it to the DA so he could get an extension on his sentence date. For some reason Reg's mother complied and Lee got his extension. I don't know how he did it but that bought him a little more time on the street.

Having his affairs in order as best he could, Lee turned himself in around December 14, 1997 to do a five year stint in a NYS prison. With Lee now gone, Big L had to step his game up. He had to make things happen for himself without the support of his big brother. Still remaining loyal to his DITC family, he reached out to them for production on his next album. He and his manager, Rich King were anxious to get the ball rolling. Rich appealed to Showbiz to set things off, but was stalled, saying he would get to Big L after his own project was done. This was unacceptable. Rich knew Big L was ready to go, so he asked Show if he would give him the green light to move forward with L's project. Showbiz gave his blessing and it was on from there with Big L and Rich getting to work immediately.

One day while walking through the hood, Big L happened upon a talented young producer by the name of Ron Browz, who was just chilling in front of his mother's building. Ron Browz's man pointed Big L out to him and urged him to holla. So he approached L and told him he made beats. Always looking to keep shit in the hood, Big L said, "Ok, lemme hear what you got." They went up to Ron Browz's mom's crib and he played a beat for L. He said, "I think I can do something with this." Big L began to spit his witty lyrics over the track and they put the recording on tape. Those were the lyrics to 'Ebonics'. Satisfied with his work, the next week Big L and Ron Browz went to D&D Studios to officially record the song. Although Rich always believed in Big L, when he heard "Ebonics," he was excited! Rich and Big L released the single as a 12" and it sold 30,000 copies almost immediately! Every DJ wanted it in their crate. Seeing the single's potential, Big L and Rich formed their independent label, Flamboyant Entertainment. Big L was on his way to the creative and financial freedom he'd always craved. The Most Valuable Poet on the M I C was back!

He got busy right away in the lab putting songs together. 'Ebonics' had created a serious buzz in the street. So much so, it caught the attention of Roc-A-Fella Records co-founder, Dame Dash. Big L and Jay-Z already had a rapport from Jay appearing on his album in '95. Along with that, and Dame being from Harlem as well, it was only natural they try to bring Big L into the fold. There was only one problem. The Roc wasn't sitting on any paper at the time. This was prior to the 'Vol 2...Hard Knock Life' success the label finally attained. Don't get me wrong, they were far from broke. But those big industry checks had not arrived just yet, so things were tight around the Roc-A-Fella offices. Negotiations were tough, but not having the money to back up the good intentions made it rougher. Rich felt The Roc was trying to sign L for nothing. After selling 30,000 copies of 'Ebonics' on their own, he needed a financial commitment from Dame. On the other side, Dame felt that Rich was in the way. Given the history he and Jay had with Big L, Dame didn't see the need for Rich to even be present at the negotiations. Dame wasn't sure of Rich's function and wanted to know what his position was in the whole scenario. He asked Rich how long the deal he had with Big L was for. Rich replied, "It's forever."

Dame said, "That's unheard of. That type of deal doesn't exist."

So he turned to Big L, and without having to ask, L said, "Like he said, it's forever." That solidified the bond between Big L and Rich even more. He could've rolled with Dame, Jay, and The Roc but instead he stayed loyal to his manager and business partner. Suffice to say, that meeting was a dud. Not long after, Dame reached out to Big L and they had a private conversation. L outlined his wishes to bring his friends, Herb McGruff and C Town along if he were to sign; but Dame was only interested in signing Big L. This presented a snag in negotiations. Big L wasn't budging and neither was Dame. L ran the conversation by a close friend to get his input and he was advised to get in the door with The Roc; then reach back and snatch his people up when he was in a better position. This made sense to Big L.

Reaching out to Dame to inform him of his change of heart Big L found that Dame had softened on his side as well, and it came to be decided that they would do a Wolfpack record, consisting of Big L, McGruff, and C Town. Bam! It was done! Big L was officially going to be in the Roc-A-Fella camp and this was an exciting time for him. All he'd worked for was finally going to be recognized and respected.

146

The Roc was very different from the stuffed shirts at Columbia; younger, and more in tune with what was going on in hip-hop, they were a perfect match for Big L's style of rap; this was cause for a celebration! Always the hustler, Big L began to organize a party to announce his signing with Roc-A-Fella. The event was to be held at Pulse, a popular night club in the 90's. Everything was falling in place for Big L; his whole life was about to change.

While everything was going in Big L's favor, something sinister was taking place on the flipside. His brother Lee was still calling shots from the pen. Lee hadn't forgotten how Black Tone shot him, leaving him with a permanent limp, and he wanted revenge. He also wanted TC and Gee out of the way while he was still locked up.

Lee used this time to plan how he could get rid of whoever would pose the most viable threat when he touched down. But out of the two, Gee was more of a hothead, so he would have to go first. But why would Lee want to hit TC and Gee? He never had any problems with either of them. Maybe it was because he feared the eminent retaliation for Reg's murder. After all, Gee was the closest to Reg at that time, and had been for the longest. But if he wasn't guilty, that shouldn't have been an issue. It makes one wonder. So what did Lee do? He linked up with a shooter from BK while doing his bid and hatched a plan to get rid of Gee, TC and Black Tone.

This was the ideal time because the hits couldn't be traced back to him as long as the shooter kept his mouth shut. The only problem was, the shooter didn't know what the three targets looked like (there was no social media back then), and they had to be pointed out to him. Their older brother Don was incarcerated at the time as well, so it left Big L to complete the task. His only job was to identify the targets, nothing more. When the shooter was released, he made

147

his way to Harlem so he could link up with L. Big L kept the shooter close until his part of the job was done. This was peculiar to people who saw the shooter and it raised eyebrows. First of all, L couldn't really explain who the hell the nigga was. All he said was it was Lee's man that he met on the inside. But to a thinking man, it was evident Lee was up to something. Why would Lee send a strange nigga from the pen to hang around L? The mf wasn't a rapper, a producer, or had any connection to the music business. So what could his function possibly be with Big L? Most people never gave it a second thought. For others it just didn't sit well, namely, Gee. He peeped Big L's movement with the dude and it made him uneasy, so he had to mind his P's and Q's on the street.

One winter day, Gee stepped out of the crib for a while to get some air. As he chilled on Lenox, he noticed the BK shooter watching him from across the Ave. Playing it cool, he kept his eye on the dude. To make sure he wasn't bugging, Gee walked to 140th St. noticing the shooter walked to 140th too, keeping his distance across the Ave. Gee walked to 142nd St to see if his man, Blind was outside. Just as he'd suspected, the shooter followed. Gee knew what time it was; he had to get that mf out of here. Blind wasn't around but Gee dipped into his building anyway to make it seem like he was going to get strapped. When he came back out, the shooter was still across the Ave. So now, instead of walking back to the block, Gee made a bee line directly toward the dude. Unzipping his jacket, he stuck his hand under his shirt as if he were reaching for his hammer. When the shooter saw Gee reach, he took off running. Gee took a couple of strides after him to see how far he would have to sell that wolf ticket. The shooter disappeared into Delano and Gee never saw him around the way again. In his mind he thought, *you f'd up Lee. You sent a lamb to do a wolf's job.* He immediately told TC and Black Tone what happened. Gee vowed to smash that mf if he ever saw him again and

148

TC told Gee to just stay off the block. Gee took his brother's advice and got low; but staying off the radar won't make your problem go away.

Gee still had to figure out what he was going to do to stay alive. He bluffed his way out of that first situation because the dude wasn't built for the job. But Gee knew Lee; that wasn't going to be the last mf he would try to send at him. He couldn't walk around with his whistle every day. That would be like begging for an all-expense paid vacation, courtesy of NYS. So what was he to do? What would you do?

Time passed and Big L was preparing for a signing party to mark his induction into the Roc-A-Fella family; that's all he talked about. Well, almost all. On February 15, 1999, Big L and two of his homies had chilled together all day, just standing around bullshitting, not doing much of anything in front of 560 Lenox Ave. As they stood in the February cold, a group of guys were also across the Ave on the downtown side standing in front of what used to be the newsstand. No one gave it a second thought because the guys were from the block. Gee being one of them. After a minute, Big L and his homies eventually decided to escape the cold by bullshitting in the supermarket on Lenox standing by the payphone acting like they were making calls just to kill time to stay someplace warm. One of Big L's homies said he needed to get his cell phone from the crib so they left the store and walked to his homie's building. Arriving, he used his man's phone to call his brother and ask him to bring the phone downstairs. As they waited in front of Building 45 in Delano Houses, a dark figure appeared from the opening in the gate on 139th St. As the man got closer, they could see he was dressed in black with a stocking cap over his face. Approaching the three men, he pulled the hammer out and motioned for the two homies to get the fuck out

149

of there, giving them a pass. He knew who the target was, and focused only on him.

The two homies took off running toward 139th St out the gate. Big L ran back toward the building and let out a scream as two shots rang out! Blaow! Blaow! The screaming stopped, but a few seconds later, another seven shots broke the silence of that winter's night! Blaow, blaow, blaow, blaow, blaow, blaow, blaow! The gunman disappeared into the dark as the two homies returned to see their friend laid out in a bloody mess.

Big L was hit nine times in the face and chest. One of the Delano police officers on patrol that night said the only thing holding his head together was his do-rag. There was no saving him. Big L was pronounced dead on the scene by police and EMTs. To say the news broke quickly would be an understatement. Crowds began to gather behind the yellow crime scene tape trying to get a glimpse of the slain rapper. Fellow DITC crew members, Fat Joe, Lord Finnesse and Showbiz were on the scene. Everyone was in disbelief. Who the fuck would want to hurt, let alone kill Big L?! The shit made no mf'n sense!

Once again, another mother would have to bury her son. Hip-hop had lost a bona-fide lyricist and we lost another NFL brother. Shock, disbelief, grief, and heartache were felt throughout Harlem. The condolences came from everywhere across the hip-hop globe. Again, those same questions arose. Who did Big L have beef with? Who were the last people to see him alive? None of it made sense because Big L wasn't really involved in street activity. To be technical, Big L was only a part of NFL by default; it was only because he was from 139th St. L never really hustled or participated in the underworld activities like the rest of us. That wasn't his lifestyle. Or, so most people thought. When I got the news I was nine months

150

into doing a three-to six-year NYS bid. The same one I was on the run from when Reg was killed. I was f'd up to say the least. My heart was broken again. I couldn't fathom a mf killing Big L. For what?! All I ever knew him to do was rap and gamble. (I was very wrong.) Who the fuck gets killed for that?! It just brought back memories of Reg getting hit.

One of the worst feelings in the world is to lose a loved one while incarcerated; you feel powerless. There's nothing a mf can do but grieve. I felt f'd up, so I can't even imagine what Lee and Don were going through. Their little brother was cut down in the street and there was nothing they could do about it. Lee definitely had to feel f'd up. His plan backfired and Big L became a casualty in his game of war. That was a hell of a price to pay. Now he had to sit with that on his conscience for the rest of his life. The family had to make preparations to lay Big L to rest.

I'll say it again, *no parent should ever have to bury their child.* It just shouldn't be that way. But in street life, it's more common than not. Big L's service was held on Saturday, February 20, 1999 at New Mt. Zion Baptist Church located on140th St between 7th and Lenox Aves. I couldn't be there of course, but I heard the service was packed with fans, friends and family who showed up to bid farewell to rap's MVP. Also amongst the throngs of people in attendance were some of hip-hop's elite including his childhood friends Ma$e, Cam'ron, the whole DITC, and a host of other celebrities. The line to pay their respects wrapped around the corner. When an immediately family member is eulogized, the DOC (Department of Corrections) will transport an inmate to either the wake or the actual funeral, as long as it takes place in NYS. So they brought Lee down from prison to attend his little brother's service. The COs escorted him down the aisle of the church, past the pews to where Big L laid in his casket. Everyone was

151

surprised how good he looked, considering the damage he had sustained. Lee stood over his brother's body and silently mourned. When the service was over, people piled in their cars making their way to George Washington Memorial Park in Paramus, NJ where Big L would forever sleep. Taken from us far too soon, he was a son, a brother, family, and friend to many.

139th Street's shining star. We miss you, bro. We love you more.

Forever Our MVP

Lamont "Big L" Coleman

1974-1999

NFL Forever

I know it was a long ride back to the CF for Lee. His heart burned with anger and revenge when what it *should* have felt was regret; deep regret for involving Big L in shit he wasn't built for. That life wasn't ever met for him. Big L was a gifted lyricist who was probably on his way to superstardom but due to his brother's twisted degenerative mind, all of that fell to the wayside. Lee let his street mentality supersede his intellect. Lee could've served his time while Big L blew up in the music business, potentially returning home to a legitimate life free from drugs, guns, murder, and prisons. I always thought the point of hustling was to better your circumstances and what could be better, than to use Big L's talent as a gateway to that life? That was Lee's ticket out of the game! I thought that was his game plan. I know it would've been mine. It's sad but we'll never know how far Big L's career would've taken him; his potential was infinite. With the love L had for hip-hop there was no limit. Such a f'n waste. Once again NFL would mourn the loss of one of our brothers.

Picking up the pieces from this one was harder than it was with Reg. Two brothers were gone in less than two years. We didn't have time to get over the first loss before taking another one but with no choice, we had to press on. Rumors started to fly through the hood about who Big L's killer was, with Gee as the prime suspect. Why? Because in the days leading up to Big L being gunned down, he'd bragged about how his brother, Lee, had sent a shooter from BK to hit Gee. If he told the wrong person, that info may have found its way to Gee's ears. If that was the case, what was he supposed to do? Of course, the right thing for Gee to do was go to the police, but we know that wasn't happening. Where we come from, calling the police goes against all codes and that definitely wasn't a mf like Gee's pedigree. As I eluded to before, the probability of the circumstances does not equal automatic guilt. I'm not saying Gee was Big L's shooter because I wasn't there. I'm also not saying he wasn't for the same reason. You can form your own opinion.

What I can't help but wonder is this: What would all the finger pointers and accusers done if they were in Gee's shoes? Perhaps he should've dismissed Big L's chatter as idle threats. That may have cost him; because the threat didn't come from L. It came from Lee. Obviously, Lee was not one to be taken lightly. It was clear he could make things happen from the pen by the first mf he sent to hit Gee. It just so happens, that dude couldn't complete the task. Knowing Lee, he wasn't going to stop there. So there was no telling what else he had up his sleeve. Would you wait around to give someone a second chance to kill you, or would you give Big L a pass because he was a rapper? His fans seem to think the latter. I wonder if those same fans would've felt that way if Big L was trying to line them up to be murdered. It's just something to think about.

153

With his name being tossed around as a suspect for the Big L murder, Gee got low for a minute. He would resurface every now and then to show his face and see what was going on around the way. On one of these occasions, while chilling on 140th St, a guy Gee was familiar with, but didn't really know approached and asked where his man, Doc was. Gee thought nothing of it and nonchalantly replied, "He was just out here. He should be back in a minute." No big deal right? Oh, but it was! It was a very big deal! Unbeknownst to Gee and everyone else, that guy turned out to be a federal agent. Those two small statements got him tangled in the web of a federal drug indictment, and he wasn't even hustling. Ultimately he would be charged with steering, or directing drug traffic for a CCE (Continuing Criminal Enterprise). But that would come later. You know how the feds operate. They build their case, and then come get you; that's what they were doing, structuring a narcotics trafficking and distribution case against NFL. Gee just happened to be there at the wrong time, opening his mouth to the wrong mf.

In the meantime, Gee did his disappearing act again and stayed out of the hood while the case was being formulated. It wasn't long before the feds pounced. In the couple of weeks after Big L's murder, the block was doing numbers. There was very little police presence, if any. Shit was sweet, or so it seemed. All the while they were being set up for the takedown. One of the workers on the block, a guy named Sike, reported to parole for a routine visit one day. His PO asked for a urinalysis, which was normal. Afterwards, he told Sike to go to a room down the hall because some people wanted to speak with him. He thought it was odd, but what could he do? Upon entering the room, he was met by a handful of police officers. One of them wore a red and black lumberjack jacket, he would never forget. They asked Sike if he had any info about guns, robberies, or murders. Of course he denied any such knowledge. As expected, they gave him a card and said if he heard anything to give them a call. When he left the parole office he threw the card away and went back uptown to the block. That was that. He thought no more about it.

On March 2nd, Sike was working his normal shift on the block when he noticed a white guy sitting in the park. Back then, any white face was automatically presumed to be the police. You just didn't see white people in the hood like that. After further examination, he recognized the man sitting in the park as the cop who wore the red and black lumberjack. Sike immediately walked through the block and warned everyone working to shut down. When he got back down the block, Doc arrived. Sike told Doc about the police being in the park. Doc looked, and sure enough the white guy was still sitting there. No sooner than Sike uttered those words, Lee's bm pulled up in the MPV. She stopped and Doc gave her some money he collected from a previous shift. He told her about the police situation and she agreed that they stay closed until shit was clear. She pulled off to pick her kids up from school. A few minutes later, as Sike and Doc stood there talking, still watching the man in the park; they turned their heads to the right and noticed the MPV coming back down the block from 7th Ave. Sike thought to himself, *What the hell she want? She just left.* But as the van got closer they saw two white males in the front seats. Sike thought, *Wait a minute. That shit don't look right.* As soon as they turned their heads back to the left, they saw federal agents armed to the teeth, running from Lenox Ave and through the park.

The agents had their machine guns and pistols drawn as they ran down on the two unsuspecting men. Sike and Doc were trapped. An agent who stood around six-foot four grabbed Sike by the shirt, pushed him against the gate and said, "We have a federal warrant for your arrest. Are you Mike Saunders?"

Sike said, "No. That's not my name." (It's not his name.)

While another agent held him there, the giant fed went to a Suburban, brought out a photo and showed it to Sike. He said, "Is this you?"

Sike looked at the picture and said, "Uh, yeah that's me."

Both men were cuffed and escorted to the MPV. When the agents opened the back door Lee's bm was in the van cuffed as well. The agent asked if she was with them, and they said no. Then the strangest thing happened. The agent took her cuffs off and released her right there on the street. Now, I don't know about you, but I've never seen anybody get released that easily. If the feds felt you were important enough to the case to cuff you, I would think they would at least take you to the Precinct to be questioned before setting you free.

You may wonder what part Lee's bm played in this whole scenario. Here's the skinny: After Reg's murder, Lee moved his operation from 139th Street to 140th because the block would be too hot. Anyone from the hood knows how the police make their presence felt after a homicide. Therefore the move was necessary. Now, I'm not saying she did anything illegal, but out of all the people around him, he trusted her the most. He knew she would do what it took to provide for their children. I can't front, she's one of those women I spoke about earlier. She was a ride or die, hold-her-man-down chick. The agents loaded the two perps into the vehicle and took them to the 32nd Precinct. Doc was under the impression that they had been arrested by TNT (Tactical Narcotics Team). This was a unit the NYPD used to flood the streets with investigators and officers who conducted buy and bust operations, arresting mostly street level dealers. Information from those arrests was passed on to other city officers and Federal anti-drug units who in turn went after higher level dealers. In the mid 80's and 90's, TNT was a force to be

156

reckoned with. They made sweeps on known drug areas, locking up anybody not wearing a badge.

TNT had niggas shook at first, but like everything else, they made a way around them. This was no TNT arrest. When Sike and Doc were brought in, agents stood up clapping and yelled, "Yay! It's NFL! We finally got NFL!"

Sike looked confused. In his mind, he thought, *NFL?! I'm not down with that shit!* And the truth is, he wasn't. But it didn't matter. They said he was, so he was! When it was time to be fingerprinted, the card the officers used was green instead of white. It read FBOP (Federal Bureau of Prisons) at the top. Now they definitely knew it wasn't a TNT bust. These were the big boys.

After being processed, Sike and Doc were placed in a holding cell while two more people on the indictment were brought in. Later, the four codefendants were taken downtown to MCC (Metropolitan Correctional Center), the federal lockup, in lower Manhattan. When they arrived the four were placed in the hole, or segregation from general population inmates. There they sat for about a week, with no details about the case. NOTHING. Then one day, an envelope was slipped under each of their cell doors. Inside the envelope on the first page it read:

The United States of America

v.

N.F.L.

In the paperwork, it named the remaining codefendants on the case and all their charges, which included drug trafficking, distribution and prostitution. Where the prostitution charge came

157

from is a mystery to me. So three more codefendants were added, including Gee and Lee's and Big L's oldest brother, Don. Gee's name on the indictment had everyone perplexed. He wasn't getting money with them, so how the hell was he involved? But the name Gerard Woodley was on the indictment as clear as day.

Now it was a waiting game to see what was going to happen next. Their first court date was a circus. When the news got out about Gee being included in the indictment, Big L's whole family showed up to court in full force, wearing "RIP Big L" t-shirts. There were other people packed in the courtroom too, just to be nosey. At some point during the hearing Big L's mother stood up and yelled, "He killed my son! Gerard Woodley killed my son!" She was going hard. This made the codefendants nervous. They were already facing federal drug charges. To put a murder on the case would make it ten times worse; her oldest son was on the indictment and that would hurt him in the long run but she didn't give a fuck. She wanted Gee to pay for Big L's murder and stopped at nothing to get it done. The court had to be called to order and Big L's mother had to be calmed down. Like I said, it was a circus.

At the end of the proceedings, the U.S. attorney notified the court that two more defendants would be present at the next date. Don and another codefendant were already in state prison and would be arrested, charged, and produced. Gee was a fugitive, and they assured the court he would be apprehended before long. While the defendants were then transported to FCI Otisville until their next court appearance, Gee had successfully managed to stay on the lam for a couple of months, but the cops were closing in. Detectives attained his beeper number from an unknown source and paged him periodically to keep tabs on his whereabouts from his return phone calls. I can't imagine whose number the cops used, but Gee answered, and that's how they were able to pinpoint his location in the Bx where he was staying with his girlfriend at the time.

On the morning of May 13th, she got up to take her son to school and everything seemed normal. When she got downstairs, she noticed an unusual amount of men who looked like cops standing in and around her building. She knew something was up. Acting like she forgot something, she doubled back to try and warn Gee, but they were on to her. They stopped Gee's girl and her son in the lobby and prohibited them from going upstairs. Having secured the girlfriend, they radioed upstairs to other officers who were already on the roof and fire escape. Upon receiving the green light, the officers busted the apartment door open. Startling Gee, who was still in bed, he tried to get to the window leading to the fire escape, but the officers were too quick, wrestling Gee to the bed and cuffing him. All he could do was put his head down and think to himself, *damn, it's a wrap.*

His days of being a fugitive were over. Gee's codefendants read about his arrest in the paper while sitting in lockup. The headline stated, 'Man Held in Big L Slay.' In the article, it stated the motive for Big L's murder was out of revenge for a longtime beef Gee had with Lee. That information was fed to the police and media by their family to conceal what actually took place. There was no way the "murder for hire" plot could get out. That would make everyone see Big L in a different light and they couldn't have that. How could sympathy be gained for the slain rapper if he had potential blood on his hands as well?

Gee's apprehension was good for the prosecution, but bad for the codefendants. When the investigation of NFL began, the feds had hopes of charging them with the RICO Law, just like The Lynch Mob. But after Reg was killed, the homicide faction of the case was nullified. With Gee now in custody and the Big L murder attached to

159

his name, the feds could up the ante. If a homicide was to be added to the case, the feds could enhance or inflate the time they offered. This had niggas shook! Even though you didn't pull the trigger, you could receive more time because the actual killer was included on your indictment. Isn't that some crazy shit?! That's what they were now facing, if Gee was found guilty of the murder charge.

Gee was brought in, questioned, and held without bail. On top of that, he had the federal drug charges to contend with. His toughest fight would be the homicide, which was the first order at hand. However, the case against him was weak. They only had hearsay to go on, and that chatter was coming from Big L's family for the most part. With no surveillance footage of Gee at the crime scene and lack of credible witnesses willing to come forward, the 2nd degree murder charge was dropped by ADA Dan M. Rather. That was a heavy-ass burden lifted off of Gee's shoulders.

Now he had the U.S. government to worry about, along with his six codefendants. One of whom was Don, Big L's oldest brother. With the murder case behind him, Gee was transported to MCC to be formally charged along with his co-defendants. After a short stay there, he was shipped to Otisville with the rest of them. As soon as Gee hit the compound and saw Sike on the walkway, he asked who on the indictment was at that spot. When he found out Don was there, he immediately reached out to his homies (Bloods) for a banger. There was no time to second guess shit. If Don was there, he needed to be prepared at all times; now, this may be a coincidence, but I think the feds tried to do them both dirty. Of all places for him to be housed, guess where they put Gee? You guessed it, right in the same dorm as Don. The tension could be felt between them. As the saying goes, you could've cut that shit with a knife.

Don had been in the jail for a couple of months, so he was settled in and knew people. Before he unpacked his setup, Gee sat on his bed to survey his surroundings and see who was who. He peeped Don moving throughout the dorm trying to get a banger and advising niggas that Gee was the mf who killed his brother; this was an attempt to gain alliances he thought he would need to go at Gee. The shit was so obvious and amusing; all he could do was look at Don and laugh to himself. But it didn't matter to Gee, because he was already strapped and ready for whatever.

Needless to say, Don's efforts were frivolous. No one wanted to get involved, so they let the two of them handle the situation man-to-man. Of course, the homies had Gee's back if shit got funky. I think Don knew this too. But regardless, they both were still on edge. That night, and every night after, neither man could get a good night's sleep as long as they were in the same unit. That had to be a f'd up feeling. Nothing became of it however, and the two men learned to coexist with one another for the time being. Besides, they had bigger fish to fry. Although Don probably hated Gee, it was in his best interest to put that beef to bed for the time being. It was all seven of them against the U.S. government.

In order for them to make the best out of the f'd up situation, they all had to be on the same page. That included Gee and Don. Going forward, the two avoided one another at all costs. Whenever the codefendants got together to discuss their case, they had to have two meetings, one with Don, and one with Gee. The only time the two would be together was for court dates, when it couldn't be prevented. It was a long battle going back and forth to court, lasting about a year. The first offer on the table for Don and Sike was 240 months, because they were labeled as career offenders due to their extensive criminal history. Others were offered ten years or less.

161

With the Big L homicide off the table, Gee's guidelines fell between three and five years. Although Gee got around the body, he still sat in a f'd up position. Having to potentially sit in prison for five years for a crew he didn't receive a single dime with was shitty in itself. But to also have a serious beef with some of them was a harder pill to swallow. That's taking one for the team at its highest form. Gee could've fought tooth and nail for his innocence, and it would've been his absolute right to do so, but he looked at the big picture and did what was best for the parties involved. Actually, everyone had to be on the same page in order for things to work out for the entire team.

While the bargaining was exchanged between the defendants and the feds, a peculiar thing occurred. Sike received word from Lee, urging him to take a plea, and if he did, Lee would have $100 sent to his account. Remember, Sike's offer was 240 months! For those who didn't do the math, that's twenty years. Sike said, "Hell no! What the fuck is $100?" And besides, he wasn't accepting any offers because it was too high. He wanted to see if the feds would lower it a little, as he should have. After all, whatever time he accepted, would have to be served by him and no one else.

Doc was offered 120 months, or ten years. He said no, as well. As things were coming down to the wire, everyone agreed they would take the lowest offers presented to them. Ultimately, the feds put sixty years on the table and told them to divide it amongst themselves. Sike was willing to take the ten years they offered, seeing how they were not going any lower. But Doc was holding out. The people told him they would give him until his birthday to make a decision. They said if he didn't take the ten offered to him, they would accept everyone else's plea and take him to trial.

162

Sure enough, on his birthday, while walking the yard, Doc heard his name over the loudspeaker telling him to report to his counselor's office. When he returned, you could see in his face how f'd up he was. Niggas asked him what happened. Doc said, "I had no choice. I had to take it. Fuck it." Ten f'n years! Collectively, they tried to spare Gee since he was the only one who was really innocent in this case. But it didn't matter. The agent threw his name in the indictment, and it was their word against his, so you know how that went.

I may be off a little, but this is how I believe the time got broken down. Three of them took eight years, which included Sike. Doc took the ten. One guy took five years. Gee took four years, along with another guy, leaving thirteen years on the table. The people were satisfied with all of the pleas. The outcome wasn't good, but at least it was over. Each codefendant knew how much time they were facing and mentally prepared themselves to do it. But a couple of things bothered them. To be honest, it makes me wonder as well. But before I proceed, let me be clear. By no means am I saying anyone was snitching. That's a bad label to attach to someone's name if you don't have absolute proof. As I've stated previously throughout these writings, I will let you, the reader, draw your own conclusion.

The first issue was, how could a guy (who shall remain anonymous) be included in eight counts on a fifteen count indictment and not even get cuffed? This mf was on video surveillance and everything, but didn't do a day in jail. How?

This next issue raises the biggest question of all: Sike asked Doc on a number of occasions how come Lee wasn't named anywhere on this indictment, if he was "The Boss." Every time he asked, Doc gave him the same response, "I don't know." Lee sat at

163

the top of the pyramid, where every federal investigation is structured from the apex down to the base. How could the entire operation be taken down and the boss go scot-free? How could that faction of NFL be under investigation and not include Lee? It makes you think, right? Has the information provided thus far caused you to ask yourself those questions? If not, let's delve deeper…

First, let me start with the fact that the federal investigation into NFL's criminal activity began in 1997, the same time when Lee caught his gun charge. Second, remember when Lee jokingly told Reg and TC about the DA offering him a deal? Was that really a joke or was it something that actually occurred? Remember when Lee asked Reg's mother for Reg's death certificate to get an extension on his sentence date? Was it really just for an extension or was it used as evidence to prove Reg's death to the DA so there would be no need for the robbery and murder faction to remain on the NFL indictment? After all, you can't put a dead man behind bars. With Reg eliminated, the feds could only go after NFL for drugs, not the robberies and murders. Maybe Lee's thinking was, *if I go down, I'm going for what I did, not another mf's shit.* Once again, I'm not saying he did it; but having Reg hit to spare himself from a RICO charge was a much stronger motive than revenge for the alleged murder of a cousin he barely knew.

Another confusing point is how the DA gave Lee an extension because he produced Reg's death certificate. I've never heard the court giving someone more time on the street to grieve the loss of a friend. If it was for an immediate family member, yes. Or, even for your grandparents. But a friend, hell no! I'm pretty sure they wouldn't even do that shit for an uncle, aunt, or cousin. But they did it for Lee.

Last, but not least, was the coup de grace in my eyes. Remember how eager Lee was for niggas to accept their pleas in the fed case? The case didn't involve Lee, so why did it matter to him whether niggas plead guilty or went to trial? The outcome had no effect on him one way or the other. Ask yourself this question: why would a mf who wasn't even named on the indictment be so desperate for niggas to cop out? That would be like me sending a kite to TI urging him to take a plea when he faced federal gun charges. I didn't have shit to do with that case. But in these good ol' United States, a defendant has a right to a trial by jury and the right to face his accusers. If one person on that indictment went to trial, anyone who snitched would've had to testify in court, revealing their identity. Once again, I'm not saying Lee or anyone else is a rat. It's not my intention to defame anyone. I'm only offering the perspective of those events as they were presented to me and how some who were on the actual case, see it. You can decide for yourself.

So the seven co-defendants received their sentences and were dispersed throughout the country to do their bids. Although Gee received one of the lesser sentences, this was probably more difficult for him than the rest of the group, because he reaped no monetary reward for the time he was about to do. It was f'd up but he took it on the chin. I don't know too much about his time in the Feds, because he didn't speak of it too much with me. We had not seen one another since '98 because I was still serving my time in NYS while all of this was going on.

I came home on work release in October of '99 when Gee was just beginning his bid, and we didn't cross paths again for a few more years. Moving forward to March or April of 2002, when Lee returned to the street after doing around four and a half years of a five year stretch, he was released with blood on his heart and a thirst for the sweet taste of revenge. Lee hit the ground running in his attempt to achieve it, letting nothing stand in his way.

Fourth Quarter

Lee's Touchdown

Twin, Stash and another guy were chilling on 139th and Lenox talking about Lee and the probability of him coming home to get on some bullshit when a van pulled up on the corner of 140th and Lenox. Twin said to Stash, "I bet that's Lee right there."

Four guys jumped out of the van, and sure enough out stepped Lee. Walking over to some guys who were out there hustling, he said a few words to them and the five men got back in the van. They made the right turn onto Lenox, drove to 139th, made the right and drove up the block. Twin wondered why Lee didn't bother to stop, but whatever. He didn't have to wonder for long because the van came back around to 139th a few minutes later and this time Lee and his people got out.

Lee approached Twin and said, "What up?"

Twin returned the greeting. Lee looked at Stash and said the same.

Stash replied, "I don't fuck with you, nigga!" Twin told him to chill.

Stash said, "Chill for what?! I don't fuck with this nigga!"

Twin pulled Stash to the side and told him to break out. After a stare off, Stash and his man walked off in the direction of his grandmother's crib. Surprisingly, Lee was uncharacteristically calm during this exchange. He just watched Stash walk away, undeniably thinking, *He's gonna be a problem for me, I see.* But that was on the back burner for now.

168

Lee directed his attention to his original motive for stopping. He needed to have a conversation with Twin. The first thing he asked was where TC and Whitey were. Twin's reply was, "I don't know. I'm out here. I can't speak for anybody's whereabouts." So they made small talk for a minute and Lee got back in the van with his people and left.

Later that night, Twin encountered one of the guys Lee had spoken to when he and the four guys hopped out on 40th earlier that day. He told Twin Lee was bugging by saying niggas couldn't be out on 40th working; and that he was taking the block back now that he was home. This guy happened to work for TC at the time. When TC got the news, he made his presence felt on the block from then on, in hopes of bumping into Lee. It never took place because they would always miss each other. This went on for a couple of days, until one night TC's bm made him go home. She was walking by 140th St and asked him, "Why are you standing out here by yourself?"

TC's response was, "I'm trying to catch up with Lee. I heard he was looking for me."

She said, "Really, you're standing out here with a gun on you, for what, to catch a case? You can handle your business and not be out here. You don't have to prove anything to anyone. When you're meant to see him, you will."

TC thought it made perfect sense, so he broke out with her and went home.

Every time Lee went around the block, niggas were MIA, and it boosted his confidence. He felt niggas were so shook, he made reference to him turning the block into a ghost town. This played right into Lee's hands. With little to no resistance, he was free to resume his activities as he pleased.

169

The next encounter Lee and Twin had was kind of eerie. Twin pulled up in 139th and saw Lee playing with Reg's sons. Reg's bm was there talking to Lee as he frolicked with the kids. The visual f'd Twin up so much, he had to sit in the car for a minute before exiting. He thought, *how could this mf have the gall to play with Reg's kids knowing what he did?* That shit was crazy to Twin but he couldn't let Lee recognize the hurt on his face.

After regaining his composure, Twin got out of the car. Of course Lee had his right hand standing guard, and the four guys he rode around with were posted up across the street by the van. As Twin approached, Lee let Reg's sons go with their mom and gave a head nod to the four dudes by the van, basically letting them know to be on point. Although Lee and Twin had no beef, Lee still took every precaution. The two men shook hands and Lee asked his right hand to step aside so they could have some privacy. Lee started the dialogue off with, "I'm hearing a lot of shit out here."

Twin said, "Likewise."

"But you can't believe everything you hear."

"That's true." Twin agreed. Lee asked Twin what he heard. Twin said, "I heard a lot. You know, I wasn't here so it's all rumor and speculation from where I'm standing." (Twin was locked up when Reg got hit) Lee asked what he thought about it. Twin continued, "I hope it's not true. But the streets are the streets and they're gonna say whatever."

Lee just nodded his head. Twin could tell the conversation was getting under Lee's skin. Lee said, "Niggas kickin dirt on my name and talkin shit about me but it was ok when Reg did what he had to do for his cousin."

Although he didn't let on, Twin knew at that moment, Lee was responsible for Reg's murder! The nigga practically admitted it! That solidified it for Twin. It was difficult, but he kept his cool as Lee shifted the conversation in another direction. Lee asked Twin where his man Rashid (Stash's uncle) was. Twin's reply was, "I don't know." Lee went on to say how he heard Rashid had something to do with Big L's murder and if any of it was true he was going to handle his business even if it meant going to Rashid's job to get it done. Word on the street was, when Big L's killer fled the scene, he went to Rashid's crib, who also lived in Delano at the time, and hid out. This fact would've made him an accessory, thereby putting his name on Lee's shit list. (I personally don't believe that theory holds any weight.)

Twin sad, "I figured you would, but like we both agreed, you can't believe everything you hear."

"At some point, you do know you're gonna have to choose a side, right?" Lee asked.

Twin responded, "I was never a dude that chose sides. I think I can get through this one standing on my side."

After some more small talk, the conversation was over. Lee's eyes peered at Twin with a look of cynicism as the two parted ways, wondering if one day he would have to add his long-time friend to his shit list. It would hurt, but so be it. After his little brother's death Lee was callous to just about everything. His *I don't give a fuck* attitude was on 10,000! In his mind, anyone could get it.

A day or so later, Lee was on 139th making his rounds when Rashid pulled up to visit his mother. He noticed Lee and his goons standing on the park side of the street and gave him the screw face while walking to the building. Lee gave Rashid the same look in

171

return. After being inside for a minute, Rashid resurfaced along with Stash's brother, his niece, and Stash himself. They all jumped in Rashid's whip and headed to 125th St. When they pulled off, Lee and his crew hopped in the van and followed. Stash noticed the van behind them and reached for his hammer, but remembered his little cousin was with them; all he could do was keep an eye on the van and watch their movement. From that first confrontation he had with Lee the plan was in effect, but after this "following" stunt, Stash really didn't give a fuck. He vowed to get Lee out of here on the very first opportunity.

Determined to complete the job, Stash went out every night with bad intentions. His girl would have to call Rashid to find Stash because he wouldn't stay in the house. Rashid would go get him, only to later receive a call saying he left the crib once again. At his wits end, Rashid would call Twin to try and talk some sense into Stash. But he wasn't having it. Stash's mind was made up.

One night Stash was leaving his grandmother's crib and Lee happened to be standing across the street with his bm and some guy. His entourage wasn't with him that night. Lee called out to Stash, "Ayo, lemme holla at you for a minute."

So Stash and his man approached Lee as his bm and the guy made their way up the block to give them some privacy. Now, there are two conflicting versions of what happened next. First, witnesses who were directly across the street say the two men spoke briefly, shook hands and parted ways. When Lee turned to walk away, Stash whipped out his hammer and shot Lee all in his back.

His bm ran back down the block screaming, "They shot Lee! They shot Lee!"

When she got to Lee's body, she quickly grabbed his gun and ran into Building 104 as the guy that was with her ran up toward 7th Ave to get out of harm's way. Stash and his man walked quickly toward Lenox and disappeared. The 2nd version goes as follows: Lee called out to Stash, same as the previous version. Stash acknowledged him and approached, asking Lee what was up.

Lee said, "I heard your uncle had something to do with my brother getting killed."

Stash said, "My uncle ain't have shit to do with that."

"Well, I'm about to start cleaning house around this mf. And when niggas start dropping, you and your uncle gon be the first to go," Lee stated with authority.

"What?" asked Stash.

Lee insisted, "You heard what the fuck I said!"

Stash said, "Yeah ok!"

In his mind, Stash thought, this shit ends right here, right now. As he spoke those two words, Stash turned to walk away and reached into his waist to grab the hammer. He spun back with the gun in his hand and when Lee saw the piece, he gave Stash a look like, *you ain't gon do shit!* Having committed himself, Stash began firing shots into Lee's chest! Blaow! Blaow! Blaow! Blaow! He was so close, Lee grabbed Stash's jacket with a death grip while a look of shock overcame his face as shell after shell penetrated his torso. Lee was so strong, Stash couldn't break free so he pulled the trigger again and again until Lee unclenched his hand; his limp body collapsing to the ground. Blaow! Blaow! Blaow! Lee's bm ran down the block screaming just like the 1st version. She grabbed his gun and ran into

Building 104. The guy with her ran up to 7th Ave. Stash and his man walked quickly toward Lenox and disappeared.

Here's the problem I have with the 1st version: if Lee was hit in the back, how did he end up on the ground face up in a spread-eagle position as witnesses say they saw him laid out on the sidewalk? The probability of him landing on his back would be slim if he took all back shots. In order for his bm to get his gun from his waist, she would've had to roll his 6ft plus, 200lb body of dead weight over onto his back. I'm not saying it's impossible, but I just don't see her doing that, especially in a frantic state of mind.

By no means am I trying to trivialize Lee's death. I only offer the two different accounts, simply because there was more than one, and I want to be as accurate as possible, as I said I would from the beginning.

Regardless of which version is precise, the fact of the matter is, we lost another NFL brother. Worse than that, his mother had to bury another one of her sons. Tragedy struck their family again and thrust them into bereavement for a second time. As usual, the news spread through the hood like germs at a daycare. I remember getting the call from Reg's girl, and I couldn't believe it. Lee was only home for about two weeks! All I could think was, *not this shit again.* This time there would be no large gathering at the hospital. There would be no outpouring of mourners. His loved ones were there but the block didn't show up like they had when Reg or Big L was killed.

Ever since Reg's death, the block had an imaginary line drawn down the center of it and like Lee predicted, niggas had chosen sides.

Sadly, this is what became of NFL. We were never the same again. TC was the only one left out of the Original Three. And even though so much controversy surrounded Lee's name, it had to hurt

174

to lose another one of his brothers. I know it hurt me, even though Lee hadn't spoken to me in five years. It just goes to show, no matter how strained a relationship may be, if you had love for someone, their demise will still have an effect on you somehow.

All the bullshit still couldn't overshadow the love niggas had for Lee. Although I wanted to pay my respects, I didn't attend Lee's wake or funeral. I believe his family would've taken it as a sign of disrespect if I'd showed up. Ever since Big L's murder, their family blamed my cousin Gee and most of them hated my family because of that, so I decided against it. I did my mourning in private; not even my wife knew my feelings at the time. All she saw was my indifference. In her eyes, I didn't give a fuck about Lee because she knew how close I was to Reg; but on the inside, I was heartbroken all over again. All the people I loved my whole life were being taken away. My NFL family was in shambles.

A few days later, Lee's family laid him to rest with his little brother, Big L in Paramus, NJ. Once again, it was a sad day for NFL. Another one of our brothers was gone.

A son, brother, father, family, and friend to many

We love you, Lee. We miss you more

Leroy "Big Lee" Phinazee

1969-2002

NFL Forever

Stash's predicament with Lee was over but his problems with the law were just beginning.

Unlike Reg and Big L's murder, there was no mystery about the identity of Lee's shooter. There were several eyewitnesses present at the time of the incident. Even if stories conflicted, no mistake could be made about who was actually there. With no mask and so many eyes on him, Stash's fate was sealed; it was only a matter of time before police caught up with him, but not before he gave them a run for their money. Stash would stay on the lam, eluding the police for close to ten months before being captured downtown at Murder Inc.'s Studio. How they closed in on him I don't know for sure, but they did.

After battling it out in court, Stash blew trial and was sentenced to thirty-three years in NYS prison, where he remains to this day.

Later that year, Gee was brought back to NYC to the FBOP halfway house in BK where he finished out the rest of his time. Unfortunately, I was on my in to do yet another bid in NYS prison. Because Gee and I wore the same size, I left him all of the clothes I'd purchased before my departure. I probably only wore shit once, so it was practically brand new. I knew he'd need them; it helps a lot when you step out the gate and have gear waiting; one less thing you have to worry about.

With incarceration behind him, Gee had the task of reintegrating back into society, which is the hard part for anyone. Don't get me wrong, doing time isn't easy by any means. Becoming a citizen of the free world after prison is more of a challenge because you have more labels attached to your name. Mama always told me I was born with two strikes against me; being black, and being a male. Add "convicted felon" to the list and it makes shit ten times worse.

This is what Gee was up against. Making the transition helps when you have support, and he always had his mom. With the obvious friction between him and Lee and Big L's family, Gee didn't parole to 139th St. This made things better for him because he wouldn't have to look over his shoulder every time he stepped outside. Gee was free again. Free to do whatever his heart desired. The question was, what would he do? He needed a job, of course, so he began his search for employment. With the stigma of an F on his report card, it made his efforts more daunting. To occupy his down time, Gee worked out to stay in shape. I remember calling home and hearing him tell me how he loved to work out to 50 Cent's 'Get Rich or Die Trying' cd that had just come out; ironic because at the time, Gee had close ties with Murder Inc. and we all know those two camps were at odds.

The bond Reg formed with Nickelz still held fast and in recent years he had become a Murder Inc. associate, bringing several of his homies with him. Nickelz made the introduction and Murder Inc. offered Gee a job. That was just the transition he needed. What better opportunity could a man coming out of the pen ask for?! That was definitely a blessing.

Working at the Murder Inc. office was Gee's first job, ever. They took a liking to Gee and rewarded him with a trip to Vegas in October 2003 to see the James Toney v. Evander Holyfield fight. When Toney stopped Holyfield in the 9th round, Gee and fans jumped for joy! His mom said she recognized him in the crowd as she watched the fight on TV. The Vegas strip was a beautiful experience for Gee. An avid boxing fan, he always longed for the chance to see a professional boxing match. To see one of his favorite fighters win by knockout was the icing on the cake. On this trip, Gee would rub shoulders with various celebrities as he partied with the

Murder Inc. entourage. Among those, happened to be Academy Award winner, Jamie Foxx, and Gee was lucky enough to snap a photo with him. He was having a ball!

It's a shame the good times with Murder Inc. were short-lived; in January of that same year, their offices were raided by the feds looking for a link to tie them with long-time friend, Kenneth "Supreme" McGriff, who stood at the helm of the Supreme Team. Authorities alleged Irv and Chris Gotti used their music money to assist Preme in cleaning his street earnings thereby disguising it as legal income. With that type of heat thrust upon the label, Murder Inc. simplified their name to "The Inc.," dropping the negative connotation that the word "murder" represented. They also felt it was best to sever ties with some of the underlings associated with the label who were on parole or had prior run-ins with the law, at least until the heat let up. I guess the Vegas trip was sort of a parting gift for them. Unfortunately, this parting of ways included Gee, bringing him back to square one as far as seeking employment. Eventually, the Gotti brothers would be acquitted of all charges on December 2nd 2005, and were free to resume business as usual. Sad to say, the label never recovered, and they failed to attain the success they'd achieved prior to the federal government dragging their names through the mud.

Once again, Gee had to fend for himself. He spent the next few months scraping by until he landed a spot in a trade school that assisted ex-offenders get jobs upon completion in the program. When he graduated, Gee began working in maintenance at an apartment complex in Newark; settling down with his girl and moving not far from where he worked; he was building a decent life for himself. Of course, he still had that street instinct and kept his ear to the ground for any chance to come up.

Living out in Jersey was good for Gee, but he wasn't the best at making friends, so he spent the majority of his time at home. Gee is my cousin and I love him to the moon and back but anyone who knew him will agree when I say, that nigga had an attitude problem. Spending extended periods of time cooped up in the crib with his girl wasn't always a good thing.

Having no social life in NJ, Gee would venture back to 139th St where his family and friends remained in order to escape the monotony. This helped relieve tension in the house, and gave his girl some space as well, but the downside was, being on the block compromised his safety.

Gee had acquired mortal enemies from the actions of his past, and his mere presence made some uncomfortable, even fearful. Shit, Big L and Lee's whole family hates me, so imagine how they must've felt when they laid eyes on Gee from time to time. It was a stressful situation to say the least. But he navigated through the tension whenever he decided to go across the bridge to enjoy himself. This went on for a few years without incident and Gee went about life enjoying his freedom. After several attempts to hold their relationship together, Gee and his girl decided to call it quits; once again he was single and ready to mingle.

Always on the prowl, he caught the attention of a young lady and the two fell hard and fast. Their romance heated up and they quickly moved in together. Things were going well, as they usually do in the beginning of all relationships but having a woman willing to match Gee's attitude and go toe-to-toe with him was a recipe for disaster. The two of them under the same roof was like holding a match to a powder keg. I'm not going to lie; Gee was a disrespectful mf at times, and she wasn't the type to concede.

179

One night, Gee and his girl got into it and to avoid the bullshit, he grabbed some of his stuff and broke out. She followed him out of the house, calling the police. The cops pulled up on the two as they were walking down the street and she went on to tell them that Gee stole her stuff out of the house. The cops asked Gee if it was true.

He said, "Officer, this is my girl. We got into it in the house. I grabbed my shit and left to avoid this nonsense."

His girl became irate, yelling, "He's lying! He stole my shit!"

The police asked Gee if they could search his bag. Handing the officer the bag, he said, "Here, go ahead."

After looking through the bag, the officer said, "Ma'am, these are all male items. What did he take belonging to you? If you're lying, we're going to lock you up for making a false report."

After hearing that she flipped the whole story and said, "He hit me! He hit me! Look at my face!"

They asked Gee if it was true. Of course he denied it. She said it again. The officers had no choice but to take Gee in, at least to separate them for the night. While he was in county lockup, Gee had someone call me to bail him out. It just so happens that at the time I was completely tapped out from paying all my bills. He was only short $100, and I can't lie, all I had was a yard. In order for me to get to him, I had to pay a toll, so when I got to him the money would've been less than the $100 he needed. I thought he would understand that if I, of all people didn't show up, I really didn't have it.

But not Gee. This nigga was too through with me. Somehow, he got out the next day and patched things up with his girl. I guess they were in love again. Gee never spoke about the incident and I didn't get a chance to explain why I couldn't get to him that night. In fact, we didn't see each other at all after he was released.

A couple of months later I got a call from TC. He said, "You know your cousin is locked up, right?"

"For what, now?" I groaned.

"A gun charge."

All I could do was shake my head. It was f'd up, but Gee carried his gun at times, depending on his gut feeling. He had to be strategic about his movement however, because people would call the police on him all the time. If he walked down the street, cops jumped out of the car and searched him. If Gee was standing on the block, or chilling in the park, they would stop and frisk him, saying he fit the description of a call they received about a man with a gun.

This last time, the caller hit pay dirt. Gee was chilling on the uptown side of Lenox Ave between 138th and 139th Sts. He had just come from walking a young lady to the train station on 135th and Lenox. Instead of going home, he went back to the block. While talking to his man, two undercover cops jumped out of the car and tried to approach Gee. As soon as he saw them he took off toward 139th and headed down to 5th Ave as the two cops gave chase. Whoever called must've mentioned how fast Gee was, because there was another car down the block waiting to trap him. With nowhere to go, Gee had no choice but to give himself up. The police arrested him and took him to the 32nd Precinct.

After receiving the call from TC, I immediately dropped $100 in Gee's account for commissary, phone calls, etc. That nigga didn't reach out to say thank you. He didn't even acknowledge receiving the

181

money! Our uncle is a CO on Rikers and coincidentally, Gee was housed in the building where he worked. Unc would pass him in the hall sometimes and Gee wouldn't even acknowledge him. Unc couldn't understand it, but that was Gee's attitude. Once he shut down, it was a wrap. When Gee finally did speak to Unc, he told him TC and I were dead to him. This threw me for a loop! He was still angry with me for not getting him out of jail that night. Gee never gave me the opportunity to explain my position in the matter. I thought it was f'd up for him to take that approach, especially with me. I've always been there for him, no matter what! I thought if anybody could get the benefit of the doubt, it would be me. But I guess not.

This put a serious strain on our relationship and I backed off from Gee altogether. Aside from his issue with me, somehow his girl got in his head and managed to turn him against the whole family. She went so far as to say TC and his own father tried to sleep with her, and Gee actually believed it! It was so bad, when his mother and father went to his court dates and the COs brought him from the back, Gee wouldn't even acknowledge them as they sat in the audience. That was crazy because anybody who's been locked up knows how it feels to step in the courtroom and see any familiar face. But Gee didn't give a fuck! He was a stubborn mf and his actions hurt his mom very deeply. She couldn't imagine what she did to make her son act that way towards her, but he did.

Gee's courtroom antics, and overall behavior towards the family went on until June of 2011 when he plead guilty and was sentenced to five years in state prison. Off he went to do his bid with no one in his corner but his girl, who would eventually leave him. Go figure. This really bothered me because I've been in prison and saw what it was like for an inmate who didn't have outside support. The state gives you the most cost effective supply of necessities that they have to. In other words, the bare minimum allowed by law. So it hurt to know my family was upstate f'd up. But just like Gee, I can be equally stubborn and I didn't feel I should give my hard earned money to someone who didn't appreciate it.

In December of 2013, I finally said enough was enough. I had to be the bigger man and resolve the issues between us, taking the trip to visit Gee at Walkill CF. It was on that visit that we put all the bullshit behind us and agreed to start anew. At the end, before I left, he asked me to tell his mother he loved her. This was a start, at least. I promised I would gladly relay the message to my aunt. Of his own doing, Gee hadn't spoken to his mother in years and I guess it was starting to eat at him. On the drive home I felt relieved; it felt good to get over our hurdle and I hoped Gee would come around to the rest of the family as well.

Two more years would pass until Gee's release in September of 2015. Upon returning, he immediately made amends with his mother and TC. I was happy for him. This was my first time seeing Gee since our visit and I actually felt bad for it. I'd fallen on hard times almost immediately after our visit and making jail trips just wasn't a priority for me. Knowing what I know now, I would've made time.

All that put to the side, I was happy for him to be home. Gee expressed his concerns about certain things and what steps he wanted to take to make things better. We talked about them briefly and made plans to link up again. Gee's outlook on life was completely opposite of what it used to be. Now more positive and pleasant to be around, he was like a new person; it was going to be totally different this time around.

183

The only negative about his return to the street was the fact that he was living on the block, something he hadn't done in years. With limited funds, Gee didn't have much of a choice; he had to stick it out until things got better for him financially. It wasn't for lack of trying. Gee passed the OSHA (Occupational Safety and Health Administration) exam in hopes of landing a job on a construction site. He was so excited when he received his OSHA card. While waiting for a job to come through, he spent his days working out and watching TV and movies with his mother, while sitting at the foot of her bed. He had a lot of making up to do, and made the best of that time with her. Gee even rekindled a romantic relationship with his son's mother who he hadn't seen in years. She lived out in Queens, so that took him away from the block from time to time, which was good. TC and Gee would take rides out to the mall with their mom trying to spend quality time that was so foolishly wasted. He was in a good space in his life and he seemed to be at peace.

Even though he had a brand new attitude, Gee always had in his mind that he was a marked man. He would make comments like, "I know niggas got money on my head. I know niggas would love to see me get dropped." It is sometimes said, people can tell when they're about to die, because they do things out of their norm. This was becoming more and more evident by Gee's abnormal behavior. He would take walks by himself, which is something he never did before. He would also be out late standing on the block for no reason. This was a no-no, but he did it nonetheless. Maybe in the back of his mind, Gee thought, *If I show people I'm not on that bullshit anymore they would live and let live.* But I guess the world wasn't ready for the new Gee.

On the night of June 23rd, Gee was standing on the corner of 139th and Lenox talking to a couple of guys from the block when he noticed one of Reg's sisters walking on her way home from work. Gee left the corner to walk her to her building, chatting her up like he usually did and they came to a stop in front of Building 106. Another chick from the block joined the conversation as the three of them shared a few laughs. Seemingly out of nowhere, a man dressed in black with a hoodie pulled tightly around his face approached Gee from behind and fired a single shot to the back of his head. Pow! Gee's lifeless body collapsed face first to the ground. When he fell, the shooter stood over Gee firing two more shots into his back. Pow! Pow! Reg's sister fell on her ass and scampered backwards on her hands and feet. She tried to get up and run, but fell again because she was wearing heels. Finally she was able to gain her balance and ran up the block yelling, "Call 911! They shot Gee! They shot Gee!"

As the scene unfolded, the shooter hurried to 7th Ave and disappeared. My aunt was in bed while her youngest son lied in the street; literally footsteps from her front door desperately clinging to life. I was at home about to go to bed when I received the call from one of my cousins that Gee had been shot. *Ok, somebody played themselves. We're gonna see how bad he's hurt. He'll recover and we'll take it from there,* I thought.

I got myself together and made my way to Harlem Hospital. I called my aunt to let her know I was on my way. No one could get in touch with TC. I called him twice, no answer. On my way to the hospital my phone rang again; this time my cousin was crying and immediately I knew. My heart sunk as he told me Gee was gone. I began hitting the steering wheel with my fist. I don't know how I was able to continue driving, but I made it to the hospital.

Upon my arrival it was pretty quiet and virtually empty with only a few strangers sitting in the waiting area. Explaining to the front desk that I was family, I was told there were already too many people inside for Gee, so I stood by the glass door until Rashid saw me and let me in. The first thing he said was, "He's gone. They couldn't save him." He tried to hug me but I pushed him away, sliding down the wall, crumpling to the floor. My mind was spinning. While the pain I felt was unbearable, the tears still didn't fall.

I got myself together and went into the room to console my aunt. I remember her saying, "I just got him back. I just got him back in my life." She sobbed quietly leaning on the table, with her head in her hands. I leaned over and kissed the back of her head, hugging her. Despite what was happening, I couldn't sit still. I stepped outside to call my mom to deliver the bad news. TC finally showed up; he went inside the room to comfort his mother. Unc got the call and arrived not long after, as people were starting to gather outside the emergency room.

About forty minutes later, the night supervisor came to the room and told my aunt she could go in the back to see Gee whenever she was ready. TC helped my aunt up and walked her back to the room where Gee laid on the table. After a few moments, the hospital staff said Unc and I could join them. When I entered the room, I saw Gee lying on the table and my aunt had her head laid on his chest. He looked as if he were asleep like I'd seen him numerous times before. She touched his face repeatedly and spoke to him quietly as if he were still here. "Gee. My Gee Love" is what she was heard saying as she sat closely to his face. Unc couldn't take it anymore and broke down crying. TC and I had to help him from the floor and sit him in a chair. TC was f'd up about his little brother but didn't show much emotion, undoubtedly trying to remain strong for his mother. We stood there and watched as my aunt doted on her youngest son. I was okay until she said his body was getting cold. That's when the grief came down on me like a ton of bricks. I touched Gee's face so I could still feel the warmth of his body, hoping it would stay that way. His body turning cold meant that he was actually dead, and that was a reality I didn't want to face. It killed me inside to see him like that. And to see my aunt in so much pain made it even worse. When he arrived, the homicide detectives escorted Gee's father to the room but he only stayed briefly because the pain was too much to bear. After a while, the Medical Examiner asked us to leave so they could take photos and then transport Gee's body to the morgue.

That night, TC took my aunt back to his house so she wouldn't have to be alone in that block or that house. Unc went home and so did I. Getting in the house at around 4am, I didn't sleep at all. Later that day my phone would not stop ringing from people expressing sympathy and sending their condolences. I appreciated the concern, but it was wearing me out to keep repeating the same thank you's over and over again. I don't know why, but I checked social media and it was all over the blogs as I knew it would be.

Ever since Big L was murdered, Gee was known to the world as his "alleged" killer. 'The Daily News' reported, "Slay Suspect Slain." They just wouldn't let that shit go. No evidence, physical or circumstantial, and they still held that shit over Gee's head. It's amazing how cruel people can be without having knowledge of the entire situation, but they jumped on the bandwagon and joined right in with the hate. I read comments like, "Karma is a bitch," and "Fuck Gee, burn in hell!" I could go on and on. There's even a Facebook page dedicated to hating him, called, "Fuck Gerard Woodley."

With so many enemies, we didn't have a clue where to begin to look for answers. Honestly, it could've come from anywhere. Unlike Reg, and Big L, Gee wasn't very well-liked. Most either didn't like him, or they feared him. Generally, it was one or the other, but people did show up for his service. For some it may have been just to

187

be nosey, but still it was a nice crowd. My aunt didn't want his service to be held in Harlem where anyone could just walk in, so the arrangements were made in The Bx at Mt. Bethel Baptist Church on July 6th. Gee was dressed in a black suit, lavender shirt and a lavender paisley tie. In the casket folded by his left shoulder was his favorite t-shirt that read, "The Man, The Myth, The Legend." It was probably the hottest day of summer, thus far and the church was filled to capacity. The service went without incident as people paid their respect to another NFL brother.

We later laid Gee to rest in Kensico Cemetery in Valhalla, NY. This loss was the most devastating for me. I love all my NFL brothers, but this one really hit home.

Once again we said goodbye to a son, a brother, a father, family and friend. We love you Gee. We miss you more.

Gerard "Gee Love" Woodley

1970-2016

NFL Forever

Cam'ron was in attendance that day and our family appreciated it. However, that caused quite a stir in the hip-hop community. People wondered how he could attend the funeral of the man who allegedly killed his long-time friend, Big L. I can't speak for him, but I will make an educated guess. Although Cam'ron wasn't a part of NFL, he knew some of the ins and outs of our lives. I also think it would be safe to say he had love for Gee as well as Big L. From where Cam'ron sits, he doesn't have to choose a side.

If one pays attention, they'll notice that most homicides are not just random acts of violence. Most of them are accompanied by a prelude, or a back-story, so to speak. Cam'ron knew the back-story of NFL's demise. And now, so do you.

The only part that remains a mystery is what happened to Gee...

Epilogue

What did we learn from these four tragedies? How does one make sense of the loss and suffering endured by the families and loved ones?

What explanation do you give children who are growing up without their fathers, and in some cases, grandfathers? Mothers and fathers who have to live without their sons? What about the countless loved ones? Did any of them really have to die?

Are we so caught up with revenge, ego and sustaining street credibility that we devalue the lives of other human beings in the process? When, if ever, does it end? It will be a vicious never-ending cycle unless everyone decides to take the high road and put the savagery to bed forever.

When you come from where we come from, that's a very difficult task. Do you exact revenge and risk your life and freedom in its name? Or do nothing and risk being looked upon as weak?

That is the mental crossroad I have traveled many a day. At some point, one must exercise the maturity necessary to rise above the madness of the streets. The youth need better examples than the ones we set before them. With most of our children approaching or already having reached adulthood, we may be too late. For the sake of everyone affected, I hope not.

There is so much more to life than what the street has to offer. I wish we would've taken heed when our mothers told us way back when. The world would probably be a better place if these four brothers were still here. Maybe there would've been time for them to change. It's heartbreaking because the allure of the street life took them away too soon.

The lust for more than what a regular job could get us was so powerful it clouded our judgment to the point where our freedom was second in line to monetary status. Disappointing our parents wasn't enough. Missing years from our children's lives and setting the poorest example as fathers wasn't enough. Nothing could stop us from seeking that ever-elusive pot at the end of the rainbow.

Some say they have no regrets for the choices they made. I can honestly say I do. I regret standing at the craps table, taking my turn, rolling the dice and entering this game of pitfalls and treachery. Choices, people. We all have them.

When asked if I would've done things differently, the answer is a vehement, YES. My experiences, along with what I've learned have shaped me to be the man I am today. I only wish I would have given myself the chance to see what my life could've been had I chosen another route.

I wonder if these four individuals felt the same somewhere along the way. We'll never know. One thing I do know is that I miss them all. I love them all. United, we stood so strong. We had that camaraderie, that brotherhood, that bond that could never be broken.

The ultimate outcome would have been very different had we all decided to walk different paths in life; ones that would've allowed us to live long and grow old together. Paths that led us far away from The Danger Zone.

Acknowledgements

First and foremost, I have to thank God for giving me the strength and fortitude to share my thoughts, feelings, and emotions and bring them to life by way of pen and paper. Well, keyboard, to be exact. I have to thank my mother for giving me life and loving me unconditionally and unselfishly through all my ups and downs. You always guided me in the right direction and kicked my behind when I steered off course. Love you infinitely, my Sunshine.

I want to thank my publishing attorney, Alan J. Kaufman for advising me along this literary journey. A special thank you goes out to Navarro W. Gray, Esq. If it wasn't for this man answering one legal question for me, the entire project would have been terminated. I appreciate you! I want to thank my editor, Sutton Mason, for putting the finishing touches on this manuscript and making it presentable to the reader. And I can't forget Aisha Linnea, who guided me through the editing and copyrighting process. I appreciate everyone's time and expertise.

I thank David Saulters, and my cousin, Thomas "TC" Riley for lending their creative talents on the artwork for this book. I'm also thankful for TC's remarkable memory; I couldn't have done it without you, Cuz! Love you, my nigga!

Tommi "GG" Curtis (my old Gucci connect) was there from the inception of this project and supported me 100%. For that I am eternally grateful. Kia Blount assisted with all of my computer questions; Lord knows I had no clue what I was doing. Thank you so much.

Lisa "Sugee Sugee" Ralston. I can't express how much our friendship means to me. No matter what I want to do, you're always there to either support me or knock me upside my head for being a dummy. I appreciate you so much for that, my Unicorn.

There's a long list of people who helped and/or supported me from the time I told them I was starting this journey. If my old brain neglects to acknowledge you it is purely by accident and please know that my heart didn't forget. Christopher Harrison, Richard "Dice" Gaynor, Drew, Anthony "Black Tone" Adams, my brothers Nairobi Washington, Anthony Cary, Harold "Took" Smith, Jame-O Wright, Alfredo "Bugsy" Lopez, Kevin "Tef" Smith, Charlie "Buck" Hvasta, Anderson "Vinylz" Hernandez, and Allen Ritter. Thank you for all your support. I love you all.

N.F.L.

Last, but definitely not least, it's an absolute "must" that I pay homage to my NFL family, for without them this project would not exist. I have to start with the Original Three, Reg (RIP), Big Lee (RIP), and TC. Then there's Big L (RIP), Gee Love (RIP), Shake, Black Tone, Don, White Tone, E Jordan, Took Da Boss, Doc, Rich Dice, Rudy, Ryer, Kenny, Tom, Shoo, Rob, and Herb McGruff.

I will always hold a special place in my heart for these brothers.

United, we were unstoppable.

Divided, we fell from grace.

But one fact still remains…

You will always be my Niggaz for Life.

N.F.L. Forever

Connect with Lou Black

Respectthepen.com

Respectthepen139@gmail.com

Instagram: Respectthepen139

RESPECT THE PEN

ORDER FORM

Quantity	Book Title	Cost	Total
	ETHYLENE	$16.00	
	SHIPPING	$ 4.95	
	Total Submitted		

MAKE CHECKS OR MONEY ORDERS PAYABLE TO:
RESPECT THE PEN, LLC
96 LINWOOD PLAZA
SUITE 405
FT LEE, NJ 07024

NAME _____
ID#_____
INSTITUTION NAME_____
ADDRESS_____
CITY_____STATE_____ZIP_____

FOR ONLINE ORDERS VISIT:
www.respectthepen.com

Printed in Great Britain
by Amazon

34272051R00116